A Bible Study By
Melissa Spoelstra

Numbers

Learning Contentment
in a Culture of More

Abingdon Press / Nashville

Numbers
Learning Contentment in a Culture of More

This book is printed on elemental chlorine-free paper.

ISBN 978-1-5018-0174-7

17 18 19 20 21 22 23 24 25 26 — 10 9 8 7 6 5 4 3 2 1
MANUFACTURED IN THE UNITED STATES OF AMERICA

CONTENTS

ABOUT THE AUTHOR

MELISSA SPOELSTRA is a popular women's conference speaker (including the Aspire Women's Events), Bible teacher, and author who is madly in love with Jesus and passionate about studying God's Word and helping women of all ages seek Christ and know Him more intimately through serious Bible study. Having a degree in Bible theology, she enjoys teaching God's Word to the body of Christ, traveling to diverse groups and churches across the nation and also to Nairobi, Kenya, for a women's prayer conference. Melissa is the author of the Bible studies *First Corinthians: Living Love When We Disagree*, *Joseph: The Journey to Forgiveness*, and *Jeremiah: Daring to Hope in an Unstable World*, and the parenting books *Total Family Makeover: 8 Practical Steps to Making Disciples at Home* and *Total Christmas Makeover: 31 Devotions to Celebrate with Purpose*. She has published articles in *ParentLife*, *Women's Spectrum*, *Just Between Us*, and the Women of Faith and Girlfriends in God blogs, and she writes her own regular blog in which she shares her musings about what God is teaching her on any given day. Melissa lives in Dublin, Ohio, with her pastor husband, Sean, and their four kids: Zach, Abby, Sara, and Rachel.

Follow Melissa:

  Twitter   @MelSpoelstra

  Instagram @Daring2Hope

  Facebook   @AuthorMelissaSpoelstra

  Her blog   MelissaSpoelstra.com
                (check here also for event dates and booking information)

INTRODUCTION

More. Something in us aches for it. We sense that there must be more than what we are experiencing. More hope. More joy. More freedom. Our culture understands this longing and offers us many suggestions. All around us people are dancing to the steps of bigger, better, faster, and more. We can easily join in the dance without even realizing it. If we just had a bigger house, a better friend, a faster phone, or more stuff, then we could be content. However, once we attain any of these things, we quickly find other areas where we lack. We find ourselves comparing and complaining without getting any closer to filling the ache inside.

God offers us another way. We must leave the world's dance moves behind and walk with Him instead. It will take intentionality as we follow His way in order to learn the art of contentment, but the benefits are definitely worth it!

Numbers may sound like an intimidating book of the Bible, but as we open its pages, we'll soon discover how relatable and relevant it is to our lives today. God led the people of Israel out of slavery and provided for their needs in the wilderness with food, water, and guidance. Yet still they grumbled. They felt the same God-shaped ache for more that we experience, but they went their own way instead of following God's instructions. Though they came so close to the land God had promised them, they were unable to enter it for forty years because of their discontent and disobedience.

In the past I found myself feeling smug and condescending toward the wayward Israelites. They wandered; they complained; they worshiped idols; they didn't respect their leaders; they doubted God. In general, they just kept going their own way. But I've discovered I don't have to look further than my own heart to find the very same tendencies.

Like the Israelites, we can start off well, but somewhere in the midst of our journeys we get tired. Just as they did, we look at our circumstances through human eyes instead of keeping our eyes on the Provider. Often we overlook God's long-term blessings when confronted with daily discomfort. We too are so close to the life of faith that God longs to give us, but we keep taking the reins, trusting only what we can see and pouting about the obstacles in the way.

The New Testament tells us that these events in Numbers were written to warn us (1 Corinthians 10:6) so that we will not make the same mistakes and suffer the same consequences. God sent His only Son to die to set us free from the sin that leads to discontentment. When we continue in it, we miss our own promised land of peace and contentment in the life He has given us. But there is good news: We can learn to be content! The Apostle Paul said in Philippians 4:11, "for I have learned how to be content with whatever I have."

In this six-week study, which begins with the opening of the Israelites' story in Exodus and quickly moves to the Book of Numbers, we will tackle some very practical topics, learning how to

- recognize our own complaining
- be content while still being authentic about the difficulties of life
- accept short-term hardship in light of the greater good of God's ultimate deliverance
- understand the relationship between complaining and worry
- change our perspective from a posture of fear to a posture of faith
- respond to opposition, scary circumstances, and even blessings in ways that cultivate contentment
- realign with God's character and promises

As we learn from the people of Israel, who got stuck wandering when they tried to do things their own way, we'll see that looking for contentment in food, stuff, and our own logic will only keep us going in circles. Just as they experienced, we'll discover that we arrive at God's promised land of peace and contentment only when we trust and obey. I pray that together we will learn lasting contentment as we discover more of our incredible God, who truly is more than enough. Only He can fill that ache inside us and help us focus on His provision and purpose in the midst of the joys and pains of life.

Options for Study

Before beginning the study, I invite you to consider the level of commitment your time and life circumstances will allow. I have found that what I put into a Bible study directly correlates to what I get out of it. When I commit to do the homework daily, God's truths sink deeper as I take time to reflect and meditate on what God is teaching me. When I am intentional about gathering with other women to watch videos and have discussion, I find that this helps keep me from falling off the Bible study wagon midway. Also, making a point to memorize verses and dig deeper by looking at additional materials greatly benefits my soul.

At other times, however, I have bitten off more than I can chew. When our faith is new, our children are small, or there are great demands on our time because of difficult circumstances or challenges, we need to be realistic about what we will be able to finish. So this study is designed with options that enable you to tailor it for your particular circumstances and needs.

1. Basic Study. The basic study includes five daily readings or lessons. Each lesson combines study of Scripture with personal reflection and application (**blue-green boldface** type indicates write-in-the-book questions and activities), ending with a suggestion for talking with God about what you've learned. On average you will need about twenty to thirty minutes to complete each lesson.

At the end of each week, you will find a Weekly Wrap-Up to guide you in a quick review of what you've learned. You don't want to skip this part, which you'll find to be one of the most practical tools of the study. This brief exercise will help your take-aways from the lessons to "stick," making a real and practical difference in your daily life.

When you gather with your group to review each week's material, you will watch a video, discuss what you are learning, and pray together. I encourage you to discuss the insights you are gaining and how God is working in your own life.

2. Deeper Study. If you want an even deeper study, there is an optional "Weekly Reading Plan" that will take you through the books of Numbers and Deuteronomy. Deuteronomy is a review of the wilderness story and will provide greater context and learning alongside the study of Numbers. You'll find the chapters for the week listed in the margin at the beginning of each week. Feel free to read them at your convenience and pace throughout the week.

Also, Digging Deeper articles are available online (see www.AbingdonWomen.com/NumbersDiggingDeeper) for those who would like deeper exploration of the text and themes; and memory verses are provided for each week of study so that you may meditate on and memorize key truths from God's Word. (Though the verses relate to the specific theme of the week, they are not necessarily from the Book of Numbers.)

3. Lighter Commitment. If you are in a season of life in which you need a lighter commitment, I encourage you to give yourself permission to do what you can. God will bless your efforts and speak to you through this study at every level of participation.

Bonus: Contentment Project Challenge. Whichever study option you choose (basic, deeper, or lighter), you also may want to participate in this bonus challenge—whether you are making an individual commitment or your group is making the commitment together. There are two parts to the commitment. First, you will wear a bracelet or wristband every day; and every time you complain (whether in your thoughts or words), you will move it to your other wrist. Whenever you do this, identify one thing in your life you are content with. If you like, you can order an adjustable "content" bracelet online at www.mudlove.com/contentment. Fifty percent of the cost of the bracelet will go directly to Visiontrust—a Christian organization that serves at-risk children in developing nations (www.visiontrust.org).

The second part of the challenge is to spend five minutes alone each day (outside if possible) listening to one worship/praise song or hymn and focusing on God's character. During this time there is no answering texts, checking e-mail, or thinking about other things; just focus on God's attributes in worship and be still.

A pilot group of over two hundred women from across the United States who participated in this challenge as I was writing the study found that the bracelet exercise and the time spent focusing on God's character significantly enhanced their contentment journey. I'll be sharing some of their feedback throughout the study.

Take time now to pray and decide which study option is right for you, and check it below. Consider also whether you plan to do the bonus Contentment Project Challenge.

___ 1. Basic Study
___ 2. Deeper Study
___ 3. Lighter Commitment
___ Bonus: Contentment Project Challenge

Be sure to let someone in your group know which option(s) you have chosen to do so that you have some accountability and encouragement.

A Final Word

As we begin this journey together, remember that the goal is not temporary behavior modification but long-term heart change. We want to begin asking different questions. When it comes to learning contentment in all things—including completing the lessons in this workbook—no longer ask yourself "How did I do?" but "Who am I becoming?" We long to be more like our Lord Jesus Christ, who spent time with the Father, was obedient, endured hardship, and cried out in prayer about the difficulty of His mission. Yet He never complained. My prayer is that as we finish this study, we will come out on the other side transformed by God and able to be content—even in a culture obsessed with more.

Melissa

Week 1

CONTENT IN DELIVERANCE

Exodus 1-15

Memory Verse

The LORD is my strength and my song;
he has given me victory.
This is my God, and I will praise him—
my father's God, and I will exalt him!
(Exodus 15:2)

Weekly Reading Plan

Numbers 1-12

DAY 1: ACCUSTOMED TO SLAVERY

Today's Scripture Focus

Exodus 1 and 3

Have you ever been so accustomed to something difficult in your life that it became the norm for you? I have friends who can't imagine life without migraines or back pain. Others have miserable marriages or children who are addicted to drugs. Life is hard for all of us. Certainly the Israelites were not immune to hardship.

Before we begin our study in the Book of Numbers, we need some background from the Book of Exodus to understand why the people of Israel ended up complaining in the wilderness. In the coming weeks we will relate with these men, women, and children who were struggling to learn contentment. So, who were they? Where did they come from? Why were they longing to go back to slavery?

The story of the Israelites began with a family that included Abraham and his son Isaac. Isaac had twin boys, and one of them was named Jacob. After Jacob wrestled with God one night, God changed his name to Israel (Genesis 32:28). The twelve tribes of Israel descended from this family had settled in the land of Canaan. When a famine ravaged the land, God had already divinely prepared a place for them in the land of Egypt through Jacob's son Joseph. The Book of Genesis ends with God's rescue of His people, who were then living in the land of Goshen in Egypt with the favor and support of Pharaoh.

However, it didn't take long before things began to change for the Israelites.

Read Exodus 1:6-14 and answer the following questions:
What changes took place in Egypt after Joseph died?

What were the concerns of the new Egyptian king regarding the Israelites?

What became the daily realities for the people of Israel?

If we were to keep reading in Exodus, we would find that a later pharaoh not only enslaved the people but even ordered that all newborn boys be killed in attempt to quell the Israelite population (1:15-22). When we begin digging into the Book of Numbers, we will find a man named Moses leading the people in the wilderness after having brought them out of slavery in Egypt. But long before he became a leader, his mother hid him in a basket as a baby in order to save him from execution.

As a mother, grandmother, aunt, sister, or friend, can you imagine the hardship and stress that every pregnant Israelite woman must have experienced? If she delivered a girl, the baby would live. Otherwise, the child that had grown in her womb for nine months would be killed. These were dark times for God's people.

According to Exodus 12:40-41, the Israelites had lived in Egypt for over four hundred years (though there are disagreements about the exact time frame in other biblical passages). Nevertheless, a world of slavery was all they were accustomed to when Moses returned to lead them out of bondage. We need to remember this history as we see the Israelites complain about God's deliverance. Getting out from under slavery would shake the status quo. It would mean venturing out into the unknown.

Like them, sometimes we must learn to accept difficult circumstances. However, when God intervenes for our rescue, we then must learn to respond with faith rather than discontent.

If you could cry out to God to deliver you from one thing or circumstance right now, what would it be?

If you were in charge of your own rescue, how would you want God to bring this deliverance?

What can be difficult for us is that often we aren't sure of what God's plan is. Is God calling us to accept tough times and learn through them, or does He want us to follow Him in faith as He makes big changes in our lives? This challenging question can foster discontentment. If God wants us to learn through our trials, we will be tempted to complain about the need to persevere. And if God says it is time for our deliverance, we may not like the changes and risks that will accompany it.

Contentment comes as we learn to listen for God's instructions and follow them because we believe He has our best interests in mind. Sometimes it's hard to reconcile that the best thing might be a wrecked car, autoimmune disorders, concussions, and fighting kids. These are the things that have hit home for me in the last few months. So, how can we know whether to sit tight and accept our circumstances or to get moving and pursue change? To help answer that, let's see how the people of Israel transitioned out of Egyptian oppression.

Read Exodus 3:1-15, and choose one of the two options below:

Draw a picture of the scene here, using speech bubbles to sum up what Moses and God said to each other:

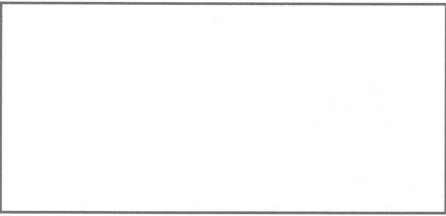

OR

Summarize the gist of this passage in 3-4 sentences:

God communicated with Moses in a *burning bush*. Boy, do I sometimes wish God would be that dramatic in giving me instruction! But for most of us, the bush doesn't burn. Even though God's instructions were difficult and Moses didn't feel qualified or excited to lead God's people, he knew what

> **Contentment comes as we learn to listen for God's instructions and follow them because we believe He has our best interests in mind.**

God was asking him to do. God said to him, "I have promised to rescue you from your oppression in Egypt. I will lead you to a land flowing with milk and honey—the land where the Canaanites, Hittites, Amorites, Perizzites, Hivites, and Jebusites now live " (Exodus 3:17). It would be a long, difficult journey, but the instructions were pretty clear.

I desire that burning bush clarity, but I can easily forget what is available to help me discern God's directions. God has not changed. He is still "I AM WHO I AM." God said to Moses, "This is my eternal name, / my name to remember for all generations" (Exodus 3:15). That includes *our* generation! God heard the cries of His people in Egypt, and He hears our cries as well. God still speaks to us today.

When I was in high school, I worried that I would not find God's will. What if I went to the wrong college or married the wrong person? My pastor at the time shared this statement that greatly helped me as I sought to listen for God's voice:

"If you do God's will, you can't help but find His will."

He explained that the Bible is full of instructions and examples of things we know are God's will for us to do:

- pray
- listen
- study His Word
- seek the Holy Spirit's help in applying God's Word
- be a part of a church community
- serve the poor
- find wisdom in a multitude of counselors

The list could go on and on. The reality is that I often neglect the things I know God has called me to do, and then I worry I won't find my way in the decisions of life. What about you? Here's what we need to remember: If we will walk closely with God, we can be assured that the great I AM will lead us.

While God has never used a burning bush in my life, He has used His Word, the counsel of others, the peace of His Spirit (or the lack thereof), experiences, and opportunities to guide me. So, if you aren't sure whether you are called to be content in your trials or content in following God to a place of deliverance, then simply start with what you do know.

Look at the bulleted list of things that are God's will above, and put a star beside anything you would like to pursue more wholeheartedly. Now spend a moment in reflection, asking God

to help you identify one action step you might take in that area in order to hear His voice more clearly.

My action step for today to do what I already know is God's will:

One time I cried out to God, asking Him what He wanted me to do, and I felt a Holy Spirit nudge when I looked up and noticed the overflowing dishes in the sink. I wanted Him to say, "Start some new project" or "Volunteer to feed the homeless." Instead, He reminded me that before I could handle more, I should start with the things I already knew needed to be done. Each of us can start with one simple act of obedience and then build on it with another and another. This will dispel our apathy and discontent as we follow God's directions one step at a time.

Let's not grow too accustomed to "slavery" as the Israelites did. God will rescue us from all of our trials, whether in this life or the next. For now, we need to listen closely for His voice so we can know what next steps to take.

Won't you join me in clinging to the great I AM and listening for His direction? As we do God's will as laid out in Scripture, we will discover God's personal will for our lives.

Talk with God

Spend a few moments focused on God's character. He is the great I AM.

Brainstorm other names for God that come to mind:

Now ask God to help you discern your next steps regarding the thing or circumstance you identified earlier, asking Him to give you contentment with His plan as He reveals it to you. If you want, write your prayer or the steps God reveals in the margin.

DAY 2: WHEN LIFE GETS HARDER

Today's Scripture Focus

Exodus 4–6

My identical twin daughters both have forms of alopecia, which is an autoimmune disorder that causes hair loss. The older twin has no hair, eyebrows, or eyelashes. She lost her hair when she was twelve years old, and now at sixteen she has grown accustomed to wigs and makeup. The younger twin started to lose hair at thirteen but has managed to keep it these past three years. A few times she has developed bald patches, and she has seen a dermatologist to receive injections in hopes of regrowth.

Recently I went with my younger daughter for injections, and for whatever reason, my mind wandered to my older daughter, thinking, "What if she were to get her hair back, too?" Pictures of her as an elementary-age girl flashed through my mind as I tried to envision what she would look like now as a young woman with hair. I quickly stopped myself from traveling too far down this path. Tears brimmed in my eyes as I fought the battle for my mind. I believe God can do anything, but I don't want to waste mental and emotional energy wishing and whining. I also know that hoping for something that isn't likely to happen can be all-consuming.

Hope deferred makes the heart sick,
*   but a dream fulfilled is*
*   a tree of life.*
*   (Proverbs 13:12)*

Read Proverbs 13:12 in the margin. Write a few sentences about a time you found this verse to ring true in your life:

We can all relate to hoping for things that haven't happened yet. Maybe we thought we were going to get a promotion, adopt a child, or get some financial relief, but it just never materialized on the timetable we expected. Our hope was deferred, and our hearts were sick. This is where we find the Israelites today. Even though they had grown accustomed to slavery, they began to hope when God sent Moses with a message of deliverance.

Even though Moses heard from God as the "I AM" in the burning bush, he still struggled with self-doubt.

Read Exodus 4:1-17 and answer the following questions:

What were Moses' concerns about telling the Israelites about God's deliverance?

How did the Lord equip and assist Moses in tangible ways?

After hearing how God would help him, how did Moses respond?

Extra Insight

"The kings of Egypt believed they were descended from the pagan god Ra, so Pharaoh thought it beneath his dignity to humble himself before the God of the Israelite slaves."[1]

The Lord called Moses to give the message of deliverance, but he wanted someone else to do it. He was not content in his calling to assist others in need of deliverance.

Describe a time when you felt that God wanted to use you to help others but you weren't excited about it:

What were some of the reasons you didn't want to get involved?

Getting involved in helping others can be scary. What if they don't want help? What if people are critical of how we serve? What if the commitment lasts longer than we anticipated?

I can think of times when I wasn't sure I wanted to get involved in ministry. When I became a small group leader for middle school students at my church, I knew it would mean sacrificing one night every week. It also meant that parents of these teens might complain about what I taught or how I led. If I decided it wasn't working out, I knew I would feel bad about stepping down. Self-doubt can keep us from the important work God has appointed us to do.

I knew God was calling me to get involved. He reminded me that He would assist me, guide me, and use me. Recently I got together with four gals who were in my small group during their middle school years and now are entering their senior year of high school. What a blessing it was to see where they are headed in life and to realize that I've played a small role in pointing them toward Christ.

How have you seen God bless you as you've gotten involved in the lives of others?

Whether it's Sunday school students, friends, people in your Bible study or small group, neighbors, or family members, God chooses to use us as His hands and feet as we help others along the path to freedom.

Moses found that, initially, the Israelites welcomed his assistance.

Read Exodus 4:29-31, and describe in a few words the reaction of the people to the message and miracles of Moses and his brother, Aaron:

Can you imagine what it must have felt like to hear that, after hundreds of years of slavery, God saw their misery and was concerned for their welfare? This is one of the ways God calls us to help one another: to remind each other that God sees and cares.

When suffering is long, we can easily lose sight of hope and forget that our God is a deliverer. But He hasn't forgotten about us. We must learn contentment in seasons of waiting, recognizing that God's plan doesn't always make sense and certainly isn't always easy. In fact, many times life seems to get more difficult just before a time of deliverance.

While the people of Israel initially welcomed Moses' message of deliverance from Egyptian bondage, they quickly changed their posture at the first sign of increased hardship. Moses and Aaron went to Pharaoh and asked him to let the people go to the wilderness to worship God for a special festival. Pharaoh responded that he didn't recognize the Israelite God and that Moses and Aaron were distracting the people from their work.

According to Exodus 5:6-9, what did Pharaoh do in retaliation for this request?

On the heels of their newfound hope that God saw and cared about them, the Israelites found that their burdens increased.

Can you think of a time when you were encouraged by God's promises but then soon found life getting harder rather than easier? If something came to mind, jot it below:

After going to a retreat or conference, I often float home on a spiritual high only to find fighting kids, a broken appliance, or something much more serious testing my faith. Contentment in deliverance means staying the course in believing God despite major setbacks. Like the people of Israel, we are likely to lose faith when things don't happen the way we thought or on the timetable we expected.

Read Exodus 5:19-23, and note the responses to the new brick quota by the following people:

The Israelite foreman's words to Moses:

Moses' words to the Lord:

The people and Moses responded with complaints when deliverance didn't come right away, and life got harder. It would have been unrealistic for them to respond with joy over having to meet new and seemingly impossible demands. But we see that God welcomes our heartbreak and disappointment. We can go to Him about our feelings with authenticity.

Listen to God's response to Moses' complaints as you read Exodus 6:1-9, and write below any information God reveals about Himself in these verses (names or character traits):

God didn't shame Moses and the people for being upset. He encouraged them to believe Him as the powerful, all-sufficient God of their ancestors. In the midst of fiery trials, God reaffirms who He is and what He will do. Through His names, God reveals His character. God was calling the people to redirect their attention from their present sufferings to His character and love.

We will never be content by focusing on our trials. Complaining doesn't actually make anything better. Complaining is like a rocking chair: It gives us something to do, but it doesn't get us anywhere. Only by shifting our focus from daily struggles to God's goodness and sovereign plan will we learn contentment through our trials. Paul reminded the church in Corinth of this very concept.

Extra Insight

"Straw was an essential ingredient in Egyptian brick making, as it was the bonding agent that held the clay together."[2]

Complaining is like a rocking chair: It gives us something to do, but it doesn't get us anywhere.

Read 2 Corinthians 4:17-18 in the margin. According to these verses, where are we to fix our gaze?

God wants us to remember that present troubles aren't forever. When we are in the midst of them, it feels as if we will never be free. No doubt that's how the Israelites must have felt. They struggled to believe God would come through for them, and God encouraged them by reminding them of His character and His promises. By calling Himself Yahweh, He was again saying, "I AM WHO I AM." I am greater than you can even imagine. Yahweh is also translated Jehovah, which means "self-existent One."[3] In other words, God isn't created, controlled, or limited. He is who He is. Not only that, but He is El Shaddai, the all-sufficient One.[4] We can trust that He will do what He says He will do, even when life circumstances are screaming the opposite. That is when we must shift our focus from all the bad that is happening to all that God is.

No one would get excited that they had to do more work in the same amount of time, deal with harsher treatment, or endure more slavery. Yet God called His people to focus on His promises rather than surrender to despair. The people had a choice to listen to God, but they refused because they were overcome with discouragement. We have all been there from time to time. Even so, God didn't give up on them. And He doesn't give up on us.

As my older twin struggled with her hair loss, I grieved along with her. At times she has become discouraged and frustrated over her condition. We've talked often about how even though we don't understand it, she can either give in to despair or focus on the good things she has in the midst of it. Those are really the only two options. Each of us faces these same choices every day.

How can you practically focus your mind on God as *Yahweh* and *El Shaddai*, rather than give in to discouragement this week? Write one or two practical ideas that will help realign your thinking:

In the Introduction I explain the Contentment Project Challenge, which is a bonus option you may choose as part of your study. In addition to wearing a bracelet that you move every time you complain, another part of the challenge is to listen to a worship song every day for five minutes, outdoors if possible. The idea is to clear away all other thoughts, be still, and worship God. Whether or not you have chosen to do this challenge throughout the study, I want to encourage you to participate in the daily worship song aspect of the challenge for the remainder of this week. (You'll find song suggestions on my website, http://melissaspoelstra.com/contentment-project/, if you are looking for some new ideas.) If you can't get outside to do this, at least get alone somewhere and focus on God for five minutes each day.

Focusing on our eternal God rather than our temporary struggles gives us perspective and hope as we grow in contentment. God's ways can be puzzling at times. His rescue doesn't usually come in the time and way we expect. So we must train ourselves to rehearse His attributes, especially in seasons when life is harder. It's a habit you'll never regret!

Talk with God

Take a few minutes right now to clear away all thoughts other than God. If possible, play a worship song or hymn, or sing one from memory. Remember that God is Yahweh—He is the Great I AM, the self-existent One, El Shaddai, the all-sufficient One. He sees your struggles and will deliver you at just the right time!

> **Focusing on our eternal God rather than our temporary struggles gives us perspective and hope as we grow in contentment.**

DAY 3: THE PRICE OF FREEDOM

Today's Scripture Focus

Exodus 7-10, 12

Can nothing ever go right? As I'm writing this, I confess I just asked that question to myself after receiving news of a large expense I hadn't anticipated. Things break, requests are denied, and at times life can feel like one struggle after another. I wonder if the people of Israel had similar thoughts when Pharaoh increased their burdens.

Some of my greatest blessings in life are my children, and the word *labor* doesn't do justice to the hours of anguish required to bring them into this world. Olympic athletes accomplish amazing athletic feats, but not before grueling hours of practice and training. Whether it's having a good marriage, developing strong character, or earning an academic degree, most accomplishments come through some sort of struggle. As we make connections between events from Scripture and our own daily lives, we find a resounding truth that many good things in life are birthed through sweat, blood, and tears.

Exodus means "exit," "departure," and is of Greek origin. The Hebrew name of the book comes from the first words of the text, "And these are the names of."[5]

Identify one or two good things in your life that have come through difficulty:

The people of Israel faced a "no" repeatedly when Moses asked Pharaoh to release them. Read Exodus 7:1-5, and write below what God said the Egyptians ultimately would know:

We find this phrase repeated throughout Scripture: "then they will know that I am the LORD." We serve a God who wants to be known. He even wanted Pharaoh to know who He is. We see this in His words to Pharaoh, spoken through Moses, regarding the plagues.

There were ten plagues in all, and many commentators couple the first nine plagues into three sets of three. The following three statements to Pharaoh were spoken at the beginning of each new set of plagues:

Before plague 1: "I will show you that I am the LORD." (Exodus 7:17)

Before plague 4: "Then you will know that I am the LORD and that I am present even in the heart of your land." (Exodus 8:22)

Before plague 7: "Then you will know that there is no one like me in all the earth." (Exodus 9:14)

The first three plagues were irritations.

Write the first three plagues below:

Exodus 7:20   1. _____

Exodus 8:2   2. _____

Exodus 8:16   3. _____

These plagues affected the entire land of Egypt. Pharaoh at first pleaded for relief, but as soon as each plague passed, he continued to refuse to allow the people to go and worship in the wilderness.

Discomfort can be a stimulant that helps us soften toward God. However, once the irritation has passed, we too often return to our own ways.

Can you identify one irritation in your life right now that God might want to use to get your attention? If so, write it below:

God longs to show us His loving character and will go the distance to get us to a place of freedom, no matter the cost.

The next three plagues were plagues of destruction. List them below:

Exodus 8:24   4. _____

Exodus 9:6   5. _____

Exodus 9:9   6. _____

Plagues seven, eight, and nine carried with them a theme of death, but the people of Israel were protected. The land of Goshen where the Israelites lived did not have to endure them.

Write these three plagues below:

Exodus 9:23-25   7. _____

Exodus 10:13-15   8. _____

Exodus 10:22-23   9. _____

Many of these supernatural events hit right at the heart of Egyptian religion. Some commentators have argued that all ten plagues corresponded to individual Egyptian gods, while others question that position. In any case, there are some connections we can make between the plagues and the false gods of Egypt:

Hapi	The god of the Nile would have been mocked by the first plague turning the water to blood.
Hekat	This goddess of childbirth had the head of a frog, and the second plague filled the land with them.
Osiris	The god of the dead, which was intimately connected with grain, would be seen as powerless when hail wiped out the crops of Egypt.
Amon-Re	The plague of darkness could be connected with Egypt's paramount sun god.[6]

One commentator offers this observation, "The entire phenomenon of the plagues certainly made a mockery of Egypt's religious system, for the pagan gods were powerless to protect their worshipers."[7] As we follow the people of Israel throughout the Book of Numbers, it will be important to remember how they have seen the Lord, Yahweh, at work in powerful ways. Not only did He strike down their oppressors, but He also shielded their own families from the worst of the plagues.

Our God is not weak. He is the one and only true God. When people make up false gods—whether out of frogs or rivers or something else from the Creator's work, such as the human spirit itself—hope in them will be disappointed. They are fakes. Only Yahweh could save the Israelite people, and only He can save us. Our slavery may look much different than theirs, but all of us have sins and struggles and circumstances that keep us in bondage. As with the Israelites, only His powerful arm can free us (Exodus 6:6). God asks that we seek Him and learn to be content with His methods and timing for our rescue.

God calls us away from counterfeits to believe what He says, even when life's circumstances scream the opposite. This isn't easy, but it is our only hope.

Read Exodus 6:6 in the margin, and take a moment to pause and remember that the God you serve has the power in His right arm to help you. Write a few words to describe God below:

"Therefore, say to the people of Israel: 'I am the LORD. I will free you from your oppression and will rescue you from your slavery in Egypt. I will redeem you with a powerful arm and great acts of judgment.'"

(Exodus 6:6)

God is committed to deliverance, and He asks us to trust Him in the process. It can be hard to understand what God is doing, but let's remember that He wants to be known. As we devote the rest of our time today to the last plague against Egypt, we will be reminded that the freedom that God offered then and offers now wasn't free. It came at a high price.

Read Exodus 12:21-30. What was the tenth plague that finally convinced Pharaoh to let the Israelites go?

What did God ask the Israelite people to do for protection against the death angel?

Why were the people to continue to observe the Passover ceremony when they entered the Promised Land?

The Passover became an observance that involved the people physically. They had to shed the blood of a lamb and apply the blood to their doorframes—an activity that didn't necessarily make sense at first. And we will see that the people annually recreated this important moment in their history so that they would not forget what God had done for them.

We too can struggle to remember how God has delivered us in the past when we are faced with new challenges.

What are some religious observances or practices that have been helpful to you in calling to mind what God has done for you?

In what way does this habit help you realign with God's ultimate truth in the midst of changing circumstances?

With the fullness of time and revelation, we know that Passover was a foreshadowing of Christ's sacrifice on the cross. Before we peek at a few New Testament passages, what connections can you make between the Passover and Jesus' death? Write anything that comes to mind below:

The New Testament sheds more insight into the relationship between Christ and Passover. In his letter to the Corinthians, the Apostle Paul urged the church to turn away from sin because, "Christ, our Passover Lamb, has been sacrificed for us" (1 Corinthians 5:7b). The prophet John the Baptist recognized Jesus as "the Lamb of God" (John 1:29), and the Apostle Peter links the lamb without defect (Exodus 12:5) with Christ, whom he calls a

God is committed to deliverance, and He asks us to trust Him in the process.

Extra Insight

Jesus entered Jerusalem five days before Passover, the time when traditionally the lamb was chosen. And, according to the first-century historian Josephus, the Passover lamb was slaughtered around 3:00 p.m. This was the exact time of day when Christ died on the cross.[8]

If we find nothing else to be content about in life right now, we certainly can come together in our appreciation that Christ has cleansed us from sin to worship the living God.

"lamb without blemish or defect" (1 Peter 1:19 NIV). And in Revelation, John the apostle sees Jesus as "a Lamb, looking as if it had been slain" (Revelation 5:6 NIV).

Now read Hebrews 9:13-15, and record below what Christ has done for us:

If we find nothing else to be content about in life right now, we certainly can come together in our appreciation that Christ has cleansed us from sin to worship the living God. He sets us free from the penalty of sin. He is saving us from the power of sin in our lives. One day, He will set us free from the very presence of sin. His blood causes judgment to "pass over" us who call on His name for deliverance. If we continue to read in Hebrews 9, we find these verses at the end of the chapter:

Just as each person is destined to die once and after that comes judgment, so also Christ was offered once for all time as a sacrifice to take away the sins of many people. He will come again, not to deal with our sins, but to bring salvation to all who are eagerly waiting for him.

(vv. 27-28)

Soak that in for a minute. Christ truly is our Passover Lamb, the perfect Son of God who gave Himself up for us. Through His blood, He gave us the greatest blessing we could ever imagine. He delivered us from the slavery of sin.

Just as God displayed His great power in Egypt through the plagues to deliver His people, He wants to rescue you through His mighty power. He is Yahweh, Jehovah, the self-existent One. And He sent His only Son to be the final sacrifice to purchase your freedom. So if you, like me, are asking today, "Can nothing ever go right?" then cling to the fact that through Christ we have salvation from sin. That certainly is something that is going right for you today, even if everything else is going wrong!

Talk with God

Spend a few minutes in prayer, telling God that you are eagerly waiting for Him. Thank Him that He is coming not to deal with our sins but to bring us salvation. While we anticipate His return, we also can rejoice in the contentment and peace He brings us in this life as we walk in close relationship with Him through the blood of Christ.

DAY 4: WHEN GOD SHOWS UP

Today's Scripture Focus

Exodus 12–14

So far we have related with the people of Israel in their bondage, struggling to believe God would do what He said He would do. God's ways are mysterious and don't always make sense to us. One moment it seems that we will be stuck with the same burdens forever, and the next we are full of faith and see deliverance on the horizon.

L. R. Knost, independent child development researcher and best-selling author, writes, "Life is amazing. And then it's awful. And then it's amazing again. And in between the amazing and awful it's ordinary and mundane and routine. Breathe in the amazing, hold on through the awful, and relax and exhale during the ordinary. That's just living heartbreaking, soul-healing, amazing, awful, ordinary life. And it's breathtakingly beautiful."[9]

Extra Insight

When the people left Egypt, Moses took the bones of Joseph with them as he had requested over four hundred years earlier (Exodus 13:19).

How can you relate to these words about having an amazing, awful, ordinary life? Identify something going on in your life that fits each of these categories:

Amazing:

Awful:

Ordinary:

Today we will find the people of Israel having some amazing experiences with God. After the Passover took place, the Egyptians couldn't get rid of them fast enough. They wanted no more of these plagues that had devastated their families.

Read Exodus 12:33 in the margin. What did the Egyptians urge the people of Israel to do, and why?

All the Egyptians urged the people of Israel to get out of the land as quickly as possible, for they thought, "We will all die!"
(Exodus 12:33)

Fill in some of the details about their departure by looking up the corresponding verse to complete the following statements:

They left without putting _____ in their bread, and they packed up their kneading boards. (Exodus 12:34)

The Israelites asked the people of Egypt to give them clothing and articles of _____ and _____. (Exodus 12:35)

There were about _____ men plus women and children who left Egypt, putting their number well over a million people. (Exodus 12:37)

Some non-Israelites accompanied the Israelites, along with their _____. (Exodus 12:38)

The Israelites did not take the main _____ ; God led them in a roundabout way to the Red Sea. (Exodus 13:17-18)

The Lord guided His people with a pillar of _____ by day and a pillar of _____ by night. (Exodus 13:21)

The Egyptians changed their _____ and decided to chase after the Israelites. (Exodus 14:5-7)

The people of Israel _____ and complained that it was better to be a slave than a corpse. (Exodus 14:10-12)

Moses encouraged the people with some words that we all need to hear when we find ourselves discontent with God's methods of deliverance. Like them, we are so prone to see things from a human perspective. I know I don't like the roundabout way that God often seems to prefer. I want the direct route, the bottom line, and deliverance on my terms.

Read Moses' words to the people below, circling any words that you need to hear in your life right now:

> But Moses told the people, "Don't be afraid. Just stand still and watch the LORD rescue you today. The Egyptians you see today will never be seen again. The LORD himself will fight for you. Just stay calm."
>
> (Exodus 14:13-14)

Later God would call His people to fight battles with physical weapons, but on this day He asked them, through Moses, to just stay calm and watch Him fight on their behalf. At this point, the Israelites were no match for the chariots and skill of an Egyptian army. Fighting would be futile. Instead God called them to stand still.

When I have panicked over financial setbacks, relational conflicts, or my children's health, I have found myself fretting over things I can't control. Can you relate? What fears have been rolling around the corners of your mind lately? One woman I know explained her understanding of the link between worry and discontentment this way: "I didn't think complaining was my issue; my issue has always been worrying. I came to realize that worry is just complaining in advance."

When we face battles that we know we cannot win, worry is just complaining in advance. In order to learn contentment, God may be asking us to believe that He will fight for us. Staying calm isn't easy when we feel like an army is chasing us, but God tells us it is possible when He is on our side.

God's very next words to Moses were, "Why are you crying out to me? Tell the people to get moving!" (Exodus 14:15). Here we see the interplay of divine sovereignty and human responsibility. We can stay calm because God will do the heavy lifting, but we must lean into Him to hear His instructions for us and then act on them in obedience.

Is there an area where God is asking you to quit talking about change so you can get moving? (For example, think about battles with food choices, exercise, prayer life, debt, anger, or time management.)

What is a first step you can take toward freedom in that area?

Moses raised his staff over the water, and God parted the Red Sea so that all of the people could pass through. Once the Israelites were safe, these same waters then drowned the Egyptian army in pursuit. God showed up in a huge way to deliver His people.

While we don't have Red Sea experiences every day—because life has a lot of ordinary and awful in the midst of the amazing—we do serve a very powerful God. He is able to part the waters to get us where He is calling us to go.

Worry is just complaining in advance.

We must remember the times when God shows up in a huge way so that during the awful and ordinary times we don't forget how amazing He is.

Can you recall a time when you saw God show up in a huge way in your life? If so, describe it below:

I remember finally getting pregnant after a miscarriage and almost two years of infertility. I even got an extra blessing when I found out we were having twins ten days before they were born. Another time one of my daughters was very sick as a five-year-old and almost died. God was so fully present with me during that time, and His Word was truly alive and active during our fifteen-day hospital stay. More recently I've seen God part the waters in helping us walk through my teen daughters' alopecia, providing for my son's college, and giving this shy girl the confidence to speak in front of crowds.

We must remember the times when God shows up in a huge way so that during the awful and ordinary times we don't forget how amazing He is.

Worship is one way we can keep God's love and power on our minds no matter what kind of day or season we are experiencing. While I was writing this study, two hundred women across the country agreed to participate in a pilot Contentment Project Challenge. As part of that challenge, each woman spent five minutes each day focusing on God's character while being still and listening to a worship song or hymn, pushing aside all invading thoughts. After the challenge ended, I received such positive feedback from the women, saying that the experience had fostered contentment in them as they praised. Worship helps us curb our complaints knowing that our powerful God is on our side. He will rescue us from whatever we are facing if we will rely on Him.

The Israelites did just that after they saw God's display of power. The Scripture says, "They put their faith in the Lord and in his servant Moses" (Exodus 14:31). Then the whole community sang a song. Imagine over a million people—and who knows how many flocks of livestock with them—worshiping God at the edge of the wilderness! I can imagine it was a sight to behold.

Read their song of deliverance in Exodus 15:1-18, and write below any words or phrases that resonate with you:

The people sang about many things, but did you notice their mention of God's right hand in verse 6? Yesterday we saw in Exodus 6:6 that God promises to use His powerful arm to deliver His people, and now His delivered people are praising His powerful right hand (15:6). When I picture God, I don't envision Him with arms and hands. We are created in His image, and we have arms and hands; so I'm not sure why I've never thought of Him that way. Whether this is a metaphor or God truly has some killer biceps, the picture of God's powerful arm and hand is repeated throughout the pages of the Bible. Let's look at just a few examples.

Circle each instance of the word *arm* or *hand,* and underline any word that denotes power:

"So the Lord *brought us out of Egypt with a strong hand and powerful arm, with overwhelming terror, and with miraculous signs and wonders."*

(Deuteronomy 26:8)

Powerful is your arm!
 Strong is your hand!
 Your right hand is lifted high in glorious strength.

(Psalm 89:13)

"I will steady him with my hand;
 with my powerful arm I will make him strong."

(Psalm 89:21)

But Lord, *be merciful to us,*
 for we have waited for you.
Be our strong arm each day
 and our salvation in times of trouble.

(Isaiah 33:2)

"O Sovereign Lord! *You made the heavens and earth by your strong hand and powerful arm. Nothing is too hard for you!"*

(Jeremiah 32:17)

By resting in God's strong arms, I know He will deliver us from whatever trials are threatening to overtake us. He is calling us to stay calm and lean hard into His strong and loving arms. Nothing is too hard for Him. He may ask us to stop standing around and get moving when the enemy presses in, but He is coming to our rescue. As we fix our minds on Him in worship, we will rediscover the awe and wonder of Yahweh's amazing power and presence!

Talk with God

Spend five minutes in worship now (let this be your time to worship with song today, if you like). Think about nothing else but God's powerful arm and hand of deliverance. If you are so inclined, write some words to your own personal song of deliverance in a notebook or journal.

Today's Scripture Focus

Exodus 15

DAY 5: NEW CHALLENGES

On the heels of God working in big ways, we often face the depressing journey of typical days or new challenges. Even though we've just seen God do something amazing in our lives, we can quickly forget His past faithfulness when we face the next setback in life.

Yesterday I mentioned that one of my daughters almost died when she was five years old. I remember the day she came home after fifteen days in the hospital. She had survived septic shock and a life-threatening blood clot. Throughout the scary days in intensive care, I had felt God's nearness and the support of the body of Christ. But when we came home, I began to be plagued by thoughts—and even dreams—such as, "What if I had taken her to the hospital sooner?" and "If only it hadn't taken the emergency room staff nine hours to figure out how serious her condition was." My logical mind knew these were useless mental pursuits, but I felt unsettled and at war within my own head. Can you relate to a time like that in your life?

The Lord had brought us through near-death challenges and walked with us as my daughter's health improved with each passing day. Yet on the other side of the trial, I hadn't expected to struggle so much, especially with thoughts that could accomplish nothing. I know fatigue and many days of stress contributed to my difficult journey, but the discontentment on the other side of God's healing work was unexpected.

If you've ever experienced unexpected struggles on the heels of God working in a big way in your life, describe it below:

This situation wasn't the only time I've felt I was in the valley right after a mountaintop event with God. I've found similar patterns in ministry, finances, friendships, marriage, and parenting. Throughout Scripture we see many similar examples in the lives of biblical characters such as Joseph, Elijah, David, and even Mary the mother of Jesus.

Yesterday we read about the Israelites' miraculous escape from Egypt with God parting the Red Sea and drowning the Egyptian army. Yet three days later, we find God's people with short-term memory loss regarding the power of Yahweh to take care of them.

Read Exodus 15:22-24. Why did the people complain?

Now before we judge them, list two or three things you have complained about this week:

Women from the pilot Contentment Project Challenge explained that often their discontent came from superficial places such as these:

- traffic
- inconveniences (someone in my way or taking up my time)
- being hot or tired
- housework
- lack of time or money
- rushed schedules
- kids fussing

One of the gals said she found a lot of her complaining surrounded slight annoyances such as family clutter or even dog hair wafting around even though she had just vacuumed the day before.

Even though the Israelites had just seen God part the waters of the Red Sea, three days without a sip of water for over a million people made for an angry mob turning against Moses. For us reading the story, it can be easy to say, "What is your problem? Can't you see that nothing is too hard for your God and that He will take care of you? He parted a sea three days ago!" I want to judge them, but then I remember how God has always taken care of my family yet I am prone to freak out over unexpected trials.

We must constantly realign ourselves with the character of God, especially when it doesn't seem He is going to come through for us. Then we can learn contentment by trusting Him to meet our needs.

We must constantly realign ourselves with the character of God, especially when it doesn't seem He is going to come through for us. Then we can learn contentment by trusting Him to meet our needs.

The people of Israel were asking the question "What are we going to drink?" when they found the water at Marah was bitter (Exodus 15:24). How would you phrase a similar question to God regarding a need in your life right now?

"Lord, _____

_____?"

Perhaps you struggled to write a question because your life is pretty smooth sailing right now. But you probably know someone close to you who has complained about circumstances in her or his life.

Recall one thing someone close to you has been venting about lately, and write it below:

According to Exodus 15:25, how did Moses respond to the people's complaint?

Whether it's our own questions or the complaints of others, we can learn from Moses to take our problems directly to the Lord. We can cry out to Him when we are thirsty, frustrated, or hit with unexpected expenses, health issues, or conflicts. When others come to us with their complaints, we can pray for their rescue. Moses couldn't fix the problem of no water, so he poured out his heart to the One he knew could help.

During the pilot Contentment Project Challenge, women were asked, for one week, to move a bracelet from one arm to the next every time they complained. Then they were to identify one thing they were content with that God had provided. As I participated in the practice of identifying my complaints, I sometimes struggled to sort out the difference between authentic statements of facts (we have no water) and complaining (I don't like this water). If you are participating in the challenge during this study, you may be having a similar struggle. But I can tell you that as time went on, the difference between facts (or needs) and complaints became more and more obvious to me.

God doesn't ask us to pretend we aren't in need. Instead, He welcomes us to cry out to Him. After all, He is all-powerful. He is Yahweh, the self-existent One. He is El Shaddai, the all-sufficient One. Through His names we remember why we should cry out to Him first. Rather than complain to our friends or family members, God asks us to present our needs to Him.

Read Philippians 4:6 in the margin and list the instructions Paul gave the church regarding our worries:

Don't _____

Instead _____

Tell God _____

Thank Him for _____

Don't worry about anything; instead, pray about everything. Tell God what you need, and thank him for all he has done.
(Philippians 4:6)

Once we've gone to God first, then we can share with others our concerns without a spirit of bitterness.

As we read the last two verses in Exodus 15, we find God revealing more about His power to the Israelites through another "I am" statement.

Read Exodus 15:26-27, and complete this statement: "I am the God who _____ you."

This is the name *Jehovah Rapha* in Hebrew. While Christians have different views about the specifics of physical healing, what we know for sure from God's name is that He has the power to heal. How and when He chooses to exercise that power can be a mystery to us at times.

God reveals Himself through Scripture so that we can learn to rely on Him. We know that He has the power to take care of all the new challenges that lie in front of us. So it can be discouraging after God delivers us in a mighty way to soon face a new situation and be in need of assistance again. We would like a little reprieve to revel in the parting of seas or the defeat of enemies. I'm sure the Israelites would have preferred that as well.

At Marah, God asked the people to do three things (Exodus 15:26):

1. Listen carefully to the voice of the LORD your God.
2. Do what is right in His sight.
3. Obey his commands and keep all His decrees.

Then He promised again that He would take care of them. Not only would He provide for them, but He also would be their healer. In the next few chapters of Exodus, we see that God miraculously fed the people with manna and quail and provided water from a rock. In chapter 20, God gave

Once we've gone to God first, then we can share with others our concerns without a spirit of bitterness.

Moses the Ten Commandments to help guide them. God promised to be with them and gave them instructions for the Tabernacle, Sabbath, and offerings. Then in Leviticus, the next book of the Pentateuch, the laws and regulations were expounded upon in detail so the people would not be unaware of God's expectations but would be equipped to listen and obey.

Just as God asked the Israelites to stay the course in trusting Him, He calls us to follow Him through the amazing, awful, and ordinary times. When they were thirsty, God used a piece of wood to sweeten the bitter waters. Then He brought them to a place with twelve springs and seventy palm trees to camp (Exodus 15:27). Whatever bitter circumstances threaten your contentment today, remember that God welcomes your cries. He longs to deliver you. He is a God who wants to be known. By revealing Himself through His names, we see that God is an all-sufficient Healer.

> Take a moment to cry out to God now. Bring Him your thirst, your hunger for justice, your problems with your leaders, your health issues, or whatever may be causing you to complain. Write your prayer below:

God calls us to fix our eyes on Him and remember His deliverance in times past to help us learn to be content with His plan.

As we embark on our study of Numbers in the coming weeks, our understanding of where the people of Israel were coming from will give us context for their journey in the wilderness. This week we saw them struggle to be content in their deliverance, complaining about these specifics of their rescue: labor, leaders, enemies, and thirst. Though they sang a song of deliverance, it only took a few days for them to express discontentment again. So, as they began their journey to the land of promise, God called them to prepare.

Seasons of waiting and preparation can be difficult times to practice contentment. Yet God calls us to fix our eyes on Him and remember His deliverance in times past to help us learn to be content with His plan.

Talk with God

End the day asking the Lord to help you grow in contentment as you meditate on Galatians 5:1: "Christ has truly set us free. Now make sure that you stay free, and don't get tied up again in slavery to the law."

Weekly Wrap-Up

As we end this week, take a moment to review what we've studied. Flip back through the lessons and write something from each day that resonated with you that you can apply in your life. I've done the first one for you as an example, though your answer may vary.

Day 1: Accustomed to Slavery

Example: <u>God's methods of rescue don't always make sense to us.</u>

_____

Day 2: When Life Gets Harder

_____

Day 3: The Price of Freedom

_____

Day 4: When God Shows Up

_____

Day 5: New Challenges

_____

Digging Deeper

Have you ever wondered about the many different names for God used throughout the Scriptures? What do we learn about God's character through names such as "I AM," El Shaddai, Jehovah, and many others? Check out the online Digging Deeper article for Week 1, "The Names of God" (see AbingdonWomen.com/NumbersDiggingDeeper) for more insight into various names used for God in the Old Testament.

VIDEO VIEWER GUIDE: WEEK 1

Contentment Clue Word: **Focused**

We learn contentment by staying focused on God and being intentional in worshiping Him.

Philippians 4:11-13 – The secret of contentment

Focusing on God's _____ rather than our ever-changing _____ is what helps us to discover contentment.

Exodus 3:12-15 and John 8:58 – Remember who God is: the great I AM

In God's plan of deliverance, sometimes things get _____ before they get easier.

Exodus 5:22-23 – Things got harder for the people of Israel

God calls us to participate in the rescue operation by _____.

Exodus 14:13-15 – God told them to get moving

Contentment is _____ _____ so that we listen to inspiration rather than spin our wheels in perspiration.

If we _____ God's will, we will _____ it.

Jude 5 – It was Jesus, the great I AM, who delivered the people of Israel

Week 2

CONTENT IN PREPARATION

Numbers 1-10

Memory Verse

May the LORD bless you
*   and protect you.*
May the LORD smile on you
*   and be gracious to you.*
May the LORD show you his favor
*   and give you his peace.*
*   (Numbers 6:24-26)*

Weekly Reading Plan

Numbers 13–23

DAY 1: TAKING STOCK OF RESOURCES

Today's Scripture Focus

Numbers 1

My son worked this past summer as a painter. One night at dinner as we were talking about his day, he mentioned that it seems like it takes almost as long to prep to paint as it does to actually get the color on the walls. His crew must clean, sand, fill holes, tape baseboards, and cover floors before they ever pop the top off a can of paint.

At times we live in seasons of preparation. These are times when God is getting us ready to do something big or enter a new season of life and ministry. When I think of preparatory times in my life, they were usually filled with waiting and mundane tasks. One of my own college summer jobs was at a retail clothing store. When the manager told us it was time to do inventory, my internal groan was loud. This is when we had to count everything in the store and record it. (The store sold baby clothes, so counting socks, onesies, and tiny clothes was tedious.) Taking stock of inventory was necessary in order to assess losses from theft and prepare for a new line of clothing to come in. It was menial and boring, yet it was a necessary preparation.

After the Israelites crossed the Red Sea, God began preparing them for the journey ahead by giving them commandments and an explanation of laws. These are found in the biblical books of Exodus and Leviticus, which precede Numbers. He also gave them instructions for the Tabernacle where He would reside.

Here's a summary of some of the instructions God gave His people:

- the Ten Commandments (Exodus 20)
- specifications for the clothing for the priests (Exodus 28; 39)
- instructions for building the altar, Tabernacle, and ark of the covenant (Exodus 30; 37; 38; 40)

- Procedures for offerings (Leviticus 1–7)
- Purification for childbirth, skin diseases, contaminated houses, and so on (Leviticus 12–15)
- Regulations for celebrations and festivals (Leviticus 16; 23–25)
- Warnings against eating blood, forbidden sexual practices, and breaking God's laws of protection (Leviticus 17–19)

God was preparing the people to live in community, and He established practices to set them up for success for the battles ahead. His laws and commands were meant to give life and protect rather than prohibit fun or freedom.

As we open the Book of Numbers this week, we find the Lord asking them to take stock of their resources. This meant counting the people. While the Hebrew name for this book of Scripture was "In the Wilderness," the English name "Numbers" came from the census we find at the beginning of the book.

Honestly, I've always thought God doesn't care as much about numbers as other things, so it's surprising to me to find an entire book with this title. We aren't supposed to measure our Christian lives by numbers, right? The Pharisees (big rule followers) in the New Testament did that. They counted how many times they prayed and fasted, and they were really big on pointing out the number of other people's faults. God wants us to live by His Spirit, which can't be measured or tacked down.

To me, pride is all about numbers: "I spent twenty minutes praying today," or "I did the dishes last time, so now it's his turn." I know that kind of counting isn't God's heart; we're supposed to have an audience of One. But I fight my nature not to get caught up in the numbers to measure success.

I also find it difficult to get hooked on a story that starts out with a bunch of statistics, as we find at the beginning of Numbers. If you find yourself having trouble getting into the story at first, too, just hold on! These numbers have great meaning. One commentator explains that "for the ancient readers of the book, such lists and numbers bore crucial insights into the very soul of their identity, their unity, their relationship to God, and their place within the community of God's people."[2] Actually, the list of people in the first chapter of Numbers invites comparison to the Book of Matthew, which begins with the genealogy of Christ. And that story certainly gets good after the list of names!

Think about all the numbers in your life: cell phone numbers, credit card or ID numbers, the time you have to be somewhere, the number of likes on the picture you posted, your bank account balance—and let's not even talk about that number on the scale. Numbers make up a part of our

identity, but they also can be sources of our discontent, especially when they don't add up the way we want them to.

While I still believe God cares about relationship more than anything else, I am learning that He uses numbers for His purposes. After all, He counted His people (Numbers 1:46), knows the number of hairs on your head (Matthew 10:30), records the number of your tears (Psalm 56:8), and asks us to forgive seventy times seven (Matthew 18:22). Numbers reveal things about our lives.

Read Numbers 1:1-4 and answer the following questions:

How long had it been since the Israelites left Egypt? (v. 1)

What did God want them to count? (vv. 2-3)

Who was to do the counting? (vv. 3-4)

Why do you think God would have wanted them to count the men of these ages?

Now skim the rest of the chapter. What was the total number of fighting men? (v. 46)

With this as the number of fighting men, some commentators have said that the actual amount of people would have been well over one million, while others have suggested it could have been more than two million.[3] The women, children, older men, and Levites would not have been included in this particular count.[4]

The last time that the number of descendants of Israel were counted was after Jacob's family joined Joseph in Egypt.

In addition, Joseph had two sons who were born in Egypt. So altogether, there were seventy members of Jacob's family in the land of Egypt.

(Genesis 46:27)

Read Genesis 46:27 in the margin. According to this verse, how many Israelites were there at that time?

Some commentators have said that for the Israelites to have multiplied from 70 to over 600,000 would have been impossible.[5] Yet the early church father John Calvin "argued against any who would deny God's miraculous ability to increase God's people from one family to over 600,000" within the time of their exile in Egypt.[6]

Regardless of their number, God was preparing Israel to go and take the land He had promised them. He wanted them to know their military strength and have everyone organized. They did it in the record speed of only twenty days (we learn this by calculating the time based on the information given in Numbers 1:1 and 10:11) because they counted in their own families and clans with well-organized leadership. Their efficient census methods and sheer numbers would bolster morale to realize they were no longer slaves but a mighty army. One source notes that "if Genesis is the book of beginnings and Exodus the book of redemption, then Numbers is the book of warfare."[7] In fact, chapter 1 in the King James Version uses the phrase "able to go forth to war" fourteen times.

The Lord also established leaders over the people to prepare the census. The census provided order, leadership, assessment of resources, and future planning.

Are there any battles or challenges looming ahead in your life? If so what are they? (Think marital, financial, relational, parental, decisions, and so on.)

Reflect for a moment to take a personal census. What resources has God made available to you to prepare for current and future battles? Consider the following:

- **Counsel from others you need to seek**
- **Prayer warriors who will pray for you**
- **Money that will be needed**
- **Time that will be required**
- **Physical or spiritual disciplines you might need to incorporate**

My resources for future battles:

God had already prepared the people by teaching them His laws and regulations for worship, food, and community life. Now He wanted them to see that a huge part of the preparation process involved realizing the value of people. In the past, the Israelites had focused on their lack— they complained about their leaders, their thirst, and the strength of their enemies. God wanted them to see that they had one another. God would be their strength, but He had multiplied them into a mighty army.

Often people can be an overlooked resource. When we are focused on our lack of resources such as money or health, we can miss the gift of people that God has put in our lives.

Who is someone God has given you as a resource in fighting your battles? Think of someone who encourages, helps, or sharpens you, and write her or his name below:

Now write a one-sentence description of how the Lord has used this person in your life to help you fight your battles:

Having the people of Israel take stock of their resources was one way God prepared them to appreciate what they had rather than what they didn't. We all can do the same. Elisabeth Elliot said, "God has promised to supply our needs. What we don't have now we don't need now."[8] This posture helps us focus on what God has provided rather than what He hasn't.

Read Numbers 1:47-54 and answer the following questions:

What tribe was not included in the census? (v. 47)

Why weren't they included? (vv. 48-49)

Extra Insight

The drastic measure of guarding the Tabernacle so that God's anger wouldn't be unleashed reminds us that God is holy. The New Testament supports the posture of reverent fear in our approach to the Father (see Acts 5:1-5; 1 Corinthians 11:27; and Hebrews 12:18-29). We also see God's grace and love throughout the Old Testament (see Exodus 34:6-7; Numbers 14:18-19; Jeremiah 31:2-3; Hosea 3:1; and Micah 7:18-19).

What were their responsibilities? (vv. 50-53)

According to verse 54, what was the people's response to these instructions?

We find here that God set some people apart for different responsibilities. We all have a role to play in serving God, and sometimes discontentment can arise when instructions are different for others than they are for us. As we take stock of our resources, we must accept that everyone isn't called to do the same things. Some of us get dressed for battle, and others carry items of worship. Each person's role may be different while retaining the same value and importance.

Treasuring the people God has put in our lives means realizing that our callings may be different. The Levites' work may have seemed special, but it involved mundane tasks such as carrying furniture and setting up poles. The warriors' training might have looked glamorous, but it meant risk of death on the battlefield.

Comparing our callings can be one of the greatest enemies to contentment. As we travel alongside our brothers and sisters in Christ, we can appreciate others, realizing that our tasks may be different but we share the common goal of embracing the promises of God.

Talk with God

Take a moment to ask God to give you eyes to see His provision of people in your life. Thank Him that during times of preparation He gives us people to fight our battles alongside us.

Treasuring the people God has put in our lives means realizing that our callings may be different.

Today's Scripture Focus

Numbers 2

DAY 2: GETTING ORGANIZED

I have a friend who likes everything in order. Her schedule, house, car, and even purse are usually neat and tidy. She knows just where to find things. I thought this might change when she had kids, but that didn't happen. She has two young boys, and in their toy room there is one bin for "cars" and another for "Disney cars." I tease her about having a disease that can be treated, but she is similar to my husband: She likes order. It is part of the way God wired her.

I, on the other hand, like to get things organized but then have trouble maintaining that order. I organize a closet or cabinet only to find within a matter of days or weeks that it is a mess again. I hate that you have to continually put things back in their assigned places.

Have you ever started a great system for organizing but ended up not sticking with it? I've started and stopped home organization systems, many different types of budgets, recipe organization, kids' chore charts, healthy eating plans, and spiritual disciplines—ideas about prayer, Scripture memory, or Bible study. All of these things started out well until I lost motivation, got sidetracked, or just couldn't keep up with all the details of the system.

Can you think of some things you have started off well but struggled to finish? List one or two below:

The Israelites had just seen God deliver them from slavery, provide a leader to guide them, and part the Red Sea in front of them. They also had a cloud to guide them by day and a pillar of fire to lead them at night. They were starting the journey full of faith and ready to obey God.

Review Numbers 1:54, which we read yesterday, and also read 2:34. What did the Israelites do in these verses?

The Israelites started off well. Like my structured friend, they found contentment in organization. As we continue on in Numbers, we will find that order and physical reminders of God's continual presence helped the people of Israel get off to a good start as they prepared for the future. Moving over a million people through a wilderness without a plan could certainly lead to chaos and discontent.

Before we get into the text, I must admit that today's passages are not touchy-feely verses that will have you underlining and putting stars next to them in your Bible. However, I don't want us to miss some great truths about God's character. We will study these two key principles from our passage today: 1) God is a God of order, and 2) God is with us.

The Israelites are headed for battle. Before they march one step or lift one sword, the Lord wants them to understand more about Him. Yahweh wanted them to see the value of making Him the center of everything they did.

Extra Insight

Fragments of Numbers were found in the caves of Qumran as part of the Dead Sea scrolls.[9]

This meant organizing the priests and making the necessary arrangements for transporting the Tabernacle for each leg of the journey.

God Is a God of Order

According to Numbers 2:1-2, what instructions did the Lord give regarding the organization of each tribe?

Now finish reading chapter 2, and fill in the diagram below to show how the tribes were organized according to family names:

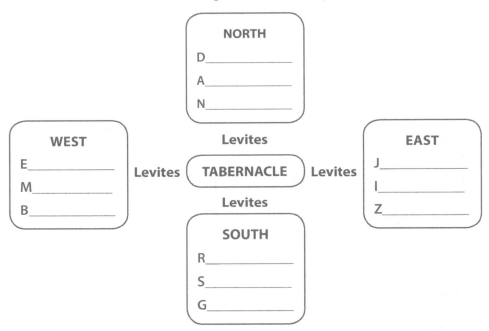

We can see throughout chapter 2 that the Lord wanted His people to set up camp and march in an orderly fashion. We also learn that believing God's promises does not mean we sit back and do nothing. One commentator writes, "God provided all the order, efficiency, and power the Israelites needed, and to him went the glory for every victory, but he did not do for them what they could and should do for themselves."[11] Likewise, as we seek the Lord, He calls us to cooperate with Him by using our human intelligence and strength as He directs. Contentment should not be confused with apathy. To be content doesn't mean that we never set goals, work hard, take risks, or use our sense to get organized. To be truly content is to use our God-given abilities in His service.

What are some benefits to an organized plan in general? (Think about work and home projects, vacation plans, and schedule management.)

Can you think of a time when you experienced discontent at the hands of disorganization? If so, describe it below:

Here are a few ideas women have shared with me:

- having to redo a project because it was damaged due to disorganization (for instance, putting a zipper in a skirt without following the directions carefully can mean having to rip it out and start all over).
- loss of time and/or money due to loss of efficiency that comes with an organized plan (for instance, a home project wastes time and money when the materials are not collected before the paid workers arrive).
- relational conflicts from poor planning (for instance, a vacation that wasn't well planned causes frustration between family members).

I can remember several occasions when I had a child in kindergarten who needed a show-and-tell item that started with the letter of the week. We would be looking around in the car on the way to school to try to find something because, truthfully, I just wasn't very organized. I often forgot to sign papers and double-booked myself for playdates with other moms. Discontentment at my lack of planning spilled over to my children whenever I forgot things. I learned that I had to write details on a calendar and live by a to-do list in order to keep everything straight.

Organization can help us with contentment so that we aren't continually dropping balls but are able to follow through on our responsibilities. While God isn't rigid, He does show us the benefits of organization. Failing to plan at times can mean planning to fail. However, since some people have more of a natural bent toward organization than others, we must not be too hard on ourselves. If we are more of a "fly by the seat of our pants" kind of person, we shouldn't compare our level of structure against that of others. What is organized for one personality type might seem like chaos to another. In addition, some seasons of life require us to modify the level of organization we can truly maintain. Toddlers, teenagers, work deadlines, or other life circumstances can put a wrench in our best laid plans for order. So, let's give ourselves grace in accordance with our particular situation.

God is not a God of disorder but of peace.
(1 Corinthians 14:33a)

Read 1 Corinthians 14:33 in the margin, and then take a few moments to consider where order may be lacking in your life. Ask God to reveal two areas where some organization and planning might bring more peace and contentment in your life:

1.

2.

I know that I need a better plan for housework and answering e-mails right now. I am praying that God will help me get more organized in these areas. It might mean delegating some responsibilities or setting a designated time to tackle these tasks. I find that usually I don't need to work harder but smarter—with an intentional plan.

The concept of organization continues throughout the next several chapters of Numbers. In fact, Numbers 7 contains eighty-nine verses explaining the offerings each tribe was required to bring. While the chapter contains much repetition, it reveals God's clarity and order in making sure everyone knew what was expected. He didn't leave them to guess what He was asking of them. In His holiness, God is shrouded in some degree of mystery, but He communicated clearly with His people what He wanted them to offer Him. He does this with us as well.

In Hebrews 10:18, we find these words, "When sins have been forgiven, there is no need to offer any more sacrifices." We no longer bring the sacrifices prescribed in Numbers 7 because of Christ's final sacrifice.

Dear brothers and sisters, I plead with you to give your bodies to God because of all he has done for you. Let them be a living and holy sacrifice— the kind he will find acceptable. This is truly the way to worship him.
(Romans 12:1)

Read Romans 12:1 in the margin. What does God ask us to offer Him?

Write a short prayer below, thanking Christ for His sacrifice on your behalf and offering yourself fully to God:

Organization is important, but again, we must remember that it is a means to an end, not an end in itself. The body of Christ is more an organism than an organization. We must remember, however, that organisms operate according to organization. The body is alive, but any biologist can explain that the nervous, skeletal, and circulatory systems function in an orderly manner. Warren Wiersbe reminds us, "If an army isn't organized, it can't fight the enemy successfully; if a family isn't organized, it will experience nothing but chaos and confusion."[12] The detail we find throughout Numbers regarding organization and planning is a reflection of the God of order we serve.

God Is with Us

Not only is God orderly, but He also is with us!

Reread Numbers 2:17, and identify what was to be placed in the middle of the traveling party:

The Tabernacle was a tangible reminder that the people of Israel were not alone. This rectangular tent consisting of curtains supported by poles was "a portable sanctuary or temple that provided a place by which God could be present in the midst of the people."[13]

Here are some fast facts about the Tabernacle from Exodus 25–26 to give you some visual details of what the people were setting up and tearing down each time they made camp:

- The Tabernacle was made from ten curtains of finely woven linen decorated with blue, purple, and scarlet thread and with skillfully embroidered cherubim. Fifty gold clasps held the curtains together to make it one continuous piece. (Exodus 26:1, 6)
- Eleven curtains of goat hair served as a covering for the tent. It also had a protective layer of tanned ram skins and a layer of fine goatskin leather. (Exodus 26:7; 14)

- A total of forty-eight frames of acacia wood and ninety-six silver bases were used to support the the Tabernacle. (Exodus 26:15-26)
- Inside were special embroidered curtains to separate the holy place from the most holy place. The ark of the covenant—containing manna, Aaron's staff, and the stone tablets (see Hebrews 9:4) was placed in the most holy place. (Exodus 26:31-34)
- A table sat outside the inner curtain and a lampstand was across the room. (Exodus 26:35)

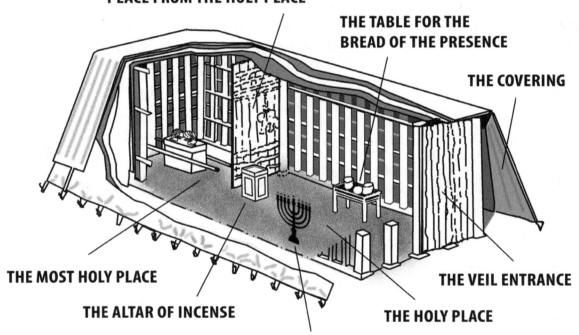

THE VEIL SEPARATING THE MOST HOLY PLACE FROM THE HOLY PLACE

THE TABLE FOR THE BREAD OF THE PRESENCE

THE COVERING

THE MOST HOLY PLACE

THE ALTAR OF INCENSE

THE VEIL ENTRANCE

THE HOLY PLACE

THE GOLDEN LAMPSTAND

The Tabernacle was a visual representation and reminder that God was with His people. About five hundred years after this account in Numbers, the more permanent temple would replace the Tabernacle as the physical home for God's presence. Then when Christ came, He fulfilled these foreshadowings of God's presence. His sacrifice made a way for God to be much closer than a tent or building among His people. Hebrews 9 and 10 give a detailed explanation of how Christ came and cancelled the old system of worship, bringing God's presence directly to each person who repents of sin and chooses to follow Jesus.

Read the following verses and write a short phrase or sentence for each, telling what we learn about the Tabernacle system in relation to the new covenant:

Hebrews 9:1, 10

Hebrews 9:13-14

Hebrews 10:1

Hebrews 10:9-10

How do these verses about what Christ has accomplished for us encourage you in the midst of any discontentment you may be feeling today?

For the Israelites, the Tabernacle was a physical container for God's presence. It was in the center of the camp so the people would have a constant reminder that God was with them. Hebrews 9:23 tells us that the Tabernacle was a copy of what is in heaven. God used the Tabernacle to help the people of Israel remember His holiness. The ritual of animal offerings, which covered sin only temporarily, pointed toward an ultimate sacrifice that would cover sin once and for all. The Tabernacle and the system it represented may be foreign to us who live under the new covenant, but we can learn from it about God's eternal desire to be near His people. God now lives within us through His Spirit rather than in a tent in our midst.

Just as Yahweh would never abandon the Israelites, He will never leave or forsake us (Deuteronomy 31:6; Hebrews 13:5). Whatever you may be experiencing right now—whether it is a season of deliverance, preparation, or difficulty—God is with you! Just as He wanted the people of Israel to make careful preparations with the Tabernacle so that they would remember His presence in their midst, He wants you to remember that because of Christ's ultimate sacrifice, He dwells within you and will never forsake you. This same God of order who lived among the Israelites is the God who lives within each of us.

Extra Insight

For further insights about why the temple system is no longer in place, read:
Luke 21:5-6;
John 2:19-21;
Acts 7:48-49;
1 Corinthians 3:16-17;
and 1 Corinthians 6:19.

Digging Deeper

In Numbers we get a glimpse of God's ideas about substitution. Check out the online Digging Deeper article for Week 2, "Substitutes" (see AbingdonWomen.com/NumbersDigging Deeper), to read more about the Levites substituting for the firstborn sons, who were required to be dedicated to the Lord. This serves as a foreshadowing to the New Testament concept of Christ as our substitute who took the punishment for our sins.

Talk with God

Take a moment to reflect on Christ's sacrifice and the closeness with God you can experience through it. Say a prayer thanking God that He is a God of order and that He is with you in your present circumstances.

Today's Scripture Focus

Numbers 3–6

DAY 3: SPECIAL SEASONS

Right now I'm taking a short break from a few things in my life for the purpose of greater focus and clarity as I study. Watching television and eating dessert aren't wrong, but for a short season I am cutting them out of my life. At night when I'm tired, I want to indulge by getting lost in a television show or having a party in my mouth with a tasty treat. Still, I must admit I feel a sense of power in saying no. It's difficult in the moment when I want it, but for the rest of the day I feel empowered by God's strength to honor my commitment. Sometimes habits or practices can control us, and abstaining for a purpose can create some space for us to hear from God.

Throughout Scripture we see examples of people in seasons of preparation who deny themselves something for the purpose of spiritual connection with God. Jesus did this as He prepared for His ministry by spending forty days in the wilderness without food (Matthew 4:1-11). Paul spoke about shaving his head to mark the end of a vow he had made (Acts 18:18).

Numbers 3–5 give more examples of God's specific organizational instructions in preparation for the journey ahead for the Israelites. If you have some extra time today, I encourage you to read all of Numbers 3–5. But if you do not have time for that, just read the following highlights:

- Aaron's four sons were ordained as priests, but two of them disobeyed God's methods for sacrifices and died in the wilderness. (3:1-4)
- The Levites were chosen to take charge of the Tabernacle and were to be substitutes for the firstborn sons who were consecrated to God. (3:5-11, 40-51)
- The Levites were registered and assigned tasks according to their family groups. (3:14-39)
- Specific instructions regarding the duties of the different Levite families and their responsibilities in caring for the Tabernacle were given for the Kohathite, Gershonite, and Merarite clans within the tribe of Levi. (chapter 4)

- Purity in the camp was very important with over one million people traveling together, so instructions were given for skin diseases and sickness. (5:1-10)
- Family life would be very important while living in such close quarters, so guidelines for accusations of infidelity were communicated clearly. (5:11-31)

These key points show us how serious the Lord was about the people following His mandates, though we see from the entirety of Scripture that God is more concerned about the heart than external rule-following. Still, in certain circumstances there is a greater need for rigidity and structure. Once the Israelites entered the Promised Land, the strict guidelines wouldn't be as necessary; but for this time of preparation, firmness was needed.

Can you think of any situations where more legalistic adherence to rules might be necessary or helpful for a specific period of time? If so, name them below:

I'm sure Olympic athletes, mothers of children with food allergies, or wedding event planners might relate to the need for inflexible plans for a certain time and place. For the Israelites in the wilderness, another situation involving legalistic rules had to do with the Nazirite vow.

Numbers 6:1-21 explains the rules for those who took the vow of a Nazirite. According to verse 2, what was the purpose of this special vow?

Extra Insight

Some commentators have suggested that both John the Baptist and James the brother of Jesus had taken Nazirite vows.

A Nazirite was a person who wanted to set themselves apart to the Lord in a special way. The English word Nazirite comes from the Hebrew word nāzîr, which means "set apart."[14] One of the most famous Nazirites in Scripture was the judge Samson. The angel of the Lord instructed Samson's mother to set him apart as a Nazirite from birth (Judges 13:5). However, as we see in Numbers, the Nazirite vow did not originate as a lifelong dedication but was intended for a period of time for intentional spiritual pursuit of God.

Extra Insight

"Jewish tradition tells us that pious women chose to become Nazirites during the Second Temple period and provides names of some of them, including Queen Helena of Adiabne and Miriam of Tadmore (Palmyra). The fact that royal women wanted to be Nazirites indicates that this status was an honored one."[15]

Refer to Numbers 6:3-8, and mark each statement below as true or false regarding someone who took a Nazirite vow:

_____ 1. They must give up wine and all other alcoholic drinks.

_____ 2. They can't go to parties or celebrate holidays.

_____ 3. They can use vinegar made from wine and drink grape juice.

_____ 4. They cannot eat raisins or grapes or anything that comes from a grapevine including the seeds or skin.

_____ 5. They must never cut their hair during the time of their vow.

_____ 6. They can't eat dessert.

_____ 7. They must not go near a dead body.

_____ 8. They can only go to a funeral if it is a close relative.

For the Nazirite vow, a person had to give up some things in order to set themselves apart to the Lord. While the Nazirite vow is not something we practice as believers today, the concept of intentionally giving up something to focus more on God is relevant to us.

The concept of self-denial—whether it be from food or drink, haircuts, or any substance or activity—can help us offer ourselves more fully to the Lord. In a culture of more, this type of practice can help us rediscover contentment through self-denial. It doesn't have to be as ritualistic as the Nazirite vow, but a small change can shake our routine enough to reset our lens on life.

Taking a special season to offer oneself to God through a spirit of fasting has been a common practice throughout Judeo-Christian history, though it is not as commonly practiced today. I know I can be prone to overcomplicate fasting or try to make it a one-size-fits-all discipline, but it doesn't have to be that way. Taking time to restrict ourselves from everyday food or drink, habits, or activities for a spiritual purpose is not only for the "super spiritual." In fact, there are many different kinds of things we might limit for a period of time (a day, week, month, or longer) to create space for more focus on God. Here are a few I've thought of:

Answers: 1) T 2) F 3) F 4) T 5) T 6) F 7) T 8) F

- a certain type of food or drink (Check with your doctor first if you have certain medical conditions or health requirements.)
- television (I regularly fast from TV because I am prone to excess in this area.)
- shopping (Commit to purchase only basic needs for a limited time.)
- eating out (Prioritize family time and see benefits for your budget as you take a season to eat only what you prepare at home.)
- social media (Unplugging for a while can clear mental space as you shift from focusing on the news of others' lives to focusing on God.)
- hobbies (If golf, crafting, collecting things, or following the lives of famous people starts taking up more time and mental energy than you'd like, a short break might give you new perspective.)
- laptops, phones, electronics (A brief respite from all things that plug into a wall can force you to walk, read, and pursue new interests.)
- complaining (Try the Contentment Project Challenge and let your complaints become a springboard to recount God's blessings, using a bracelet as a reminder.)

I'd like to fast from laundry, cooking, and cleaning as well, but I know that those are not the things I am predisposed to overdo. Maybe you do need to take a break from home projects or obsessive cleaning. We find the most benefit when we take a break from the particular things we are inclined to do in excess. For some it may be playing online games, checking certain apps on their phone, devoting obsessive attention to world news, or checking e-mail too frequently.

What other things would you add to the list?

Is there a specific thing that God is calling you to consider taking a break from now? If so, write it below:

Continue reading Numbers 6:9-12, and answer the following questions:

What was a Nazirite to do if they defiled themselves by being near a dead body? (vv. 9-10)

What would be the result of these actions? (v. 11)

What must the Nazirite do next? (vv. 11-12)

Instead of giving up when we hit the first bump in the road, God calls us to rededicate ourselves to Him and press on.

When it comes to fasting or abstaining, God knows there will be times when breaking our vow might be out of our control. While He is a God of order, He knows that sometimes life interferes with our best-laid plans. Instead of giving up when we hit the first bump in the road, God calls us to rededicate ourselves to Him and press on.

Rather than presenting an animal offering as the Nazirite did, we can recall Christ's final sacrifice that cleanses and purifies us when we don't live up to every goal we set. God's grace allows us to fail forward in our pursuit of offering ourselves more fully to Him, even if it is imperfectly. Instead of having an "all or nothing" attitude that prevents us from making commitments, we can commit to a special season of fasting knowing that when we slip, like the Nazirites we can lean into the offering and rededicate ourselves to God.

Is there a commitment you've made to God—whether recently or in the past—where you feel you've been missing the mark? Write a short prayer below, asking God to cleanse and purify you; then express your rededication to following Him:

Knowing that perfection isn't expected when it comes to commitments, is there an area where you can "begin again" when it comes to spiritual rhythmns?

The next section in this chapter reminds us that the Nazirite vow was not a lifelong pursuit. It had a start date and an end date.

Read Numbers 6:13-21, and summarize below the instructions for ending the Nazirite vow. (If you are feeling artistic, you can draw a picture of some of the offerings and the prescribed haircut.)

Extra Insight

"Like ancient Nazirites, modern laypersons who belong to the 'priesthood of all believers' can dedicate themselves to God and enjoy a holy experience with him in their personal spiritual lives."[16]

God instructed the Nazirite to mark the end of this special season with rituals to formalize that it was over. Similarly, setting an appropriate end time for your fast will be important as you offer yourself to the Lord. If you have never done any sort of self-denial for the sake of spiritual focus, I encourage you to start with a reasonable timeframe. For example, you might stay off social media or not eat chocolate for one day, or you might be ready to deny yourself for a week or two. Or perhaps you might just say that for the next hour you want to offer no complaints of any kind—mental or verbal—and say only positive things. I encourage you to take some time right now to ask God how long He is calling you to offer yourself to Him by abstaining from the thing you identified above.

Of course, it may be that this is not the right season in your life for any kind of fast, and that is OK. Whenever I have tried to abstain from something with only limited focus, I've found it difficult to follow through. Remember that the people of Israel were in a season of preparation. When you sense that God is doing a work within you, that is the time when fasting and vows take on special meaning.

Whenever I'm at a crossroads, whether I'm seeking direction from God or broken over the illness of a family member or friend, an intensity drives me toward the Lord in my fast. Other times I've sensed God calling me to make a physical restriction for a time of spiritual preparation.

As you consider the purpose and timing for a season of intentional reduction or fasting, you might ask yourself questions such as these:

- Do I need direction from God regarding an approaching decision?
- Is someone close to me suffering physically, emotionally, or mentally and in need of prayer?

- Might some area of excess be distracting me from wholehearted devotion to God?
- Is God preparing me for a particular task or calling?

Ask the Holy Spirit to lead you as you seek intimacy with God. Remember that empty spiritual practices and rote religious routines are not His thing, but a genuine desire to know God more can transform your life!

Talk with God

Spend some time talking and listening to God, asking for more clarity regarding a possible season of fasting in your life. Fill in the blanks below as you are able:

I sense the Lord is leading me to abstain from _____

_____ for a season to set myself apart to God in

a special way starting on _____ and ending on

_____. As a result of this fast, I hope to

_____.

If you don't hear anything specific regarding a special time of focus, you don't have to make something up. Perhaps God knows your time of preparation is coming soon, or He may remind you of what you've learned about the Nazirite vow at some time in the future.

Today's Scripture Focus

Numbers 6 and 9

DAY 4: BLESSINGS

One day my husband was on the phone with a friend who was telling him of a new ministry opportunity she had. When he got off the phone, he said to me, "She is exactly the right person for that job. Her amazing gifts and talents are going to bring so much creativity and enthusiasm to that ministry." I asked him why he was telling me instead of her. He immediately redialed the number and spoke those very words to this gal. I know they brought her much encouragement and blessing.

Take a minute to think about the power of words in your own life. What is a compliment someone has given you in the past that has stuck with you?

Some of us may struggle to think of words of blessing we have received because our memories are overwhelmed with negative comments or criticism. Today we will find that even if no one else has spoken a blessing over us, God has!

From the very beginning, God has blessed His creation, calling it good. And He continues to shower us with ongoing blessings. In Scripture we find fathers, such as Isaac in Genesis, putting great emphasis on the blessing they would pass on to their sons. You may recall that Isaac's son Jacob dressed up to look and smell like his twin brother, Esau, in order to steal the blessing of the firstborn. As we see in Numbers 6, there are two aspects of blessing: speaking the blessing and celebrating the blessing.

Speaking the Blessing

Right after God talks about the Nazirite vow, He inserts a glimpse of Himself as a "Blesser." This passage has been called the Lord's Prayer of the Old Testament.

Take a moment to read Numbers 6:22-27, and write the content of the three blessings below:

May the Lord _____

_____ *(v. 24)*

May the Lord _____

_____ *(v. 25)*

May the Lord _____

_____ *(v. 26)*

According to verse 27, God said that every time Aaron and his sons pronounced this blessing, He Himself would bless them. In the midst of a book about a lot of numbers, God's order, and strict consequences for disobedience, we see also that God longs to bless us. His rules and discipline were for the community's benefit in the wilderness.

Which one of the following blessings could you especially use in your life right now? Circle the one that stands out to you:

Protection   God's smile and gracious acts   Favor and peace

To gain greater understanding into the meaning of the words *gracious* and *peace*, let's look at the Hebrew roots:

The Israelites found comfort for generations in these words found in Numbers 6:22-27. "An abridged form of the priestly blessing" was found on "two small amulets of silver leaf" found in "a cave overlooking the Hinnom valley outside the ancient city of Jerusalem."[19]

"To be gracious…is not merely to smile; it is to show favor in the form of beneficial action."[17]

"Peace (*šālôm* [*shalom*] in Hebrew) means more than the absence of war. It means well-being, health, prosperity and salvation: in short, the sum total of all God's good gifts to his people."[18]

God instructed His people to speak and pray blessings over one another. You may not have grown up receiving verbal blessings from your family or knowing that God loves you and longs to bless you. And if that was your experience, my heart goes out to you. The withholding of a blessing can plant seeds of insecurity and discontent. But even if you didn't hear words of blessing in your formative years, you can choose to be a giver of blessings to those in your sphere of influence out of the overflow of God's blessings to you.

Gary Smalley and John Trent say this in their book *The Blessing*: "We shouldn't look down and lose hope if we grew up without the blessing. We should look up, instead, to the incredible provision of a blessing that can leave our lives overflowing, the kind of blessing that can even replace a curse with contentment."[20]

Your family, friends, coworkers, and neighbors need to hear you speak blessings into their lives. It's easy to see the bad in people. They might be late, sloppy, or irritating. However, if you strain your eyes to look for the good, you will surely find it. Initiative, kindness, honesty, and so many other good qualities are waiting to be noticed and affirmed. In fact, we need to speak blessing into the lives of those around us even when they think they don't need it. We must tell them over and over the amazing gifts and potential we see in them. Even if we have to look hard to find the good amidst their annoying habits or unkind behaviors, we must speak it out. It will bring them encouragement, and we might discover our own contentment growing in the process.

Is there someone the Lord is bringing to mind who needs some blessing from you? If so, write their name in the blessing from Numbers 6:24-26:

> May the LORD *bless* _____
>   *and protect* _____.
> May the LORD *smile on* _____
>   *and be gracious to* _____.
> May the LORD *show* _____ *His favor*
>   *and give* _____ *his peace.*

Your family, friends, coworkers, and neighbors need to hear you speak blessings into their lives.

Take time today to call, write, text, or go to this person and speak a blessing in their life. Tell them what you prayed for them. Be specific about what you see in them and how God wants to bless them. If possible, stop and do this now. If that's not possible, write the details of the blessing you are planning below:

Who:

When:

How:

What I plan to say:

The words of the godly are a life-giving fountain.
(Proverbs 10:11a)

The tongue has the power of life and death.
(Proverbs 18:21, NIV)

Celebrate the Blessing

Not only did God want His people to speak blessing to one another; He also instructed them to take time for regular celebrations to remember His blessings in their lives. God knows us intimately. The psalmist said of God, "He knows how weak we are; / he remembers we are only dust" (Psalm 103:14). Because the Lord knows of our tendency to forget, He asks us to set aside special times to remember what He has done.

Counting our blessings is one of the greatest ways to restore contentment when we get into complaining mode. When we are unhappy that our washing machine is broken, we can remember that we have clothes to wash. In times when we feel that we are wandering in circles, we can look back and remember how God has directed us in the past.

The Lord had passed over the Israelites' homes in Egypt when the plague of death claimed all firstborn sons because of Pharaoh's stubbornness, and He has delivered them out of slavery. And during their season of organization in the wilderness, He didn't want them to forget their deliverance. Can you relate to forgetting God's past rescue in the midst of seasons of preparation? Let's discover how God called Israel to remember His blessings.

Read Numbers 9:1-5 and write below what the people were to celebrate:

Counting our blessings is one of the greatest ways to restore contentment when we get into complaining mode.

Now turn to Leviticus 23:4-8 and answer the following questions:

What other festival began on the day after the Passover? (v. 6)

What needed to be stopped during the first day of the festival? (v. 7)

What must be presented to the Lord during this celebration? (v. 8)

How many days was the celebration? (v. 8)

How would you summarize some important elements in God's instructions about celebrating the festivals of Passover and Unleavened Bread? Write a few ideas below:

Though we are not under the mandate to celebrate Passover as new covenant Christ-followers, the concept of remembering God's blessings in times of celebrations echoes into our lives as well.

What are some holidays or special times when you stop to remember God's blessings?

How do those celebrations give you time and space to reflect on what God has done?

I will admit that sometimes I can become consumed with preparations, travel, and activities during holidays such as Easter or Christmas, causing me to lose time for reflection. God's festivals were about stopping ordinary work, gathering with others in community for holy assembly, and recounting God's blessings.

As you consider an upcoming time of spiritual celebration, what practical changes could you make to better implement the practice of recounting God's blessings? (Try to think of at least one.)

Whether we decide to attend a special gathering with other believers or scale back on regular work to focus on God, we must be intentional about remembering.

Turn again to Numbers 9. As you skim through verses 6-12, you'll find that some of the men were ceremonially unclean because they had come into contact with a dead body. They asked Moses what to do, and I love Moses' response!

What did Moses say in Numbers 9:8?

Moses didn't respond with human wisdom. Instead he sought the Lord with each new question or concern. We can learn from Moses to continually go back to the Lord with each new situation or problem that presents itself in our lives.

In Numbers 9:9-11, we see that God told Moses that anyone who was ceremonially unclean or away during Passover could celebrate one month later. This reveals again that God is holy and serious about instructions yet flexible and gracious when we humbly come to Him. He longs for us to stop and celebrate so that we can remember all He has done.

In Numbers 9:13-14, God reminded the people of the importance of stopping to remember. He said that unless they had a good reason, such as the men who were unclean, failing to observe Passover would mean being cut off from the community.

This seems harsh to me given my modern mind-set, but it reminds me that the Lord knows us. He understands that failing to remember His blessings will lead to discontentment, especially in long seasons of preparation. And He wants us to know that speaking blessings to one

Extra Insight

"Over 150 times in the book of Numbers it's recorded that God spoke to Moses and gave him instructions to share with the people."[21]

another and remembering God's deliverance are vital. Whether or not it's the time of year for celebrations of holy remembrance, I encourage you to end your time today reflecting on God's blessings in your life.

Talk with God

Spend some time reflecting on Christ's sacrifice on the cross so that judgment would be "passed over" in your life. Thank God for that blessing right now, and recall the many other ways He has blessed you. If you are alone, speak out loud what He has done for you, and ask Him to help you speak blessings into the lives of those around you. If others are in earshot, you can pray silently or write a prayer in the margin.

Today's Scripture Focus

Numbers 8–10

DAY 5: LIGHTS AND REST STOPS

When my children were in elementary school, they loved to play a game with neighborhood friends called flashlight tag. Once during this game, one of my daughters fell and cut her knees and palms. (Clearly she was not the one with the flashlight!) As I cleaned her up and tried to calm her down, I asked her how she got hurt. She said she tripped over some uneven pavement in the sidewalk because it was so dark that she couldn't see. She was wandering through the dark front yard trying not to get caught by the light.

Have you ever found yourself there spiritually? You know, you are wandering aimlessly in the dark, but you just don't feel like getting caught by the light of conviction. It exposes too much. It might mean giving up a bad habit you enjoy, forgiving people who have hurt you, or giving up your discontentment over what God has or has not provided. I know I've been there.

We know the light is better, but sometimes we want to wander in the dark just a little longer and go our own way. When we wander too long, God mercifully lets us hit some pavement to bring us back into the light.

Extra Insight

The first ten chapters of the Book of Numbers cover only fifty days and "describe how Moses organized Israel for the march from Sinai to the promised land."[22]

Read Numbers 8:1-4, and fill in the blanks below to complete some truths about God's light in the Tabernacle.

There were _____ lamps.

They were to be placed so their light shined _____.

The lampstands were made out of _____.

They built them exactly how _____ told them to.

Light is an analogy God uses often to help us understand His character. In Numbers 8, God tells Aaron to place the lamps so that the light shines forward. In the same way, we are to let the light of God's Word and His Spirit shine forward in our lives, illuminating our way.

Look up the following verses related to light, and write a short summary of each:

2 Samuel 22:29

Psalm 18:28

Matthew 5:14-16

John 8:12

1 John 1:5

To live in the light is to live intentionally. It is to walk in the bold assurance that even in the darkness of this world, God is lighting the way for us as we follow Him (see Psalm 139:12).

Read Leviticus 24:2-4 in the margin. What did the oil lamps in the Tabernacle require, and how often did they have to be refilled?

Like the lamps in the Tabnernacle, we need a constant flow of energy or life in order to shine—a continual filling of the Holy Spirit. For us, this continual filling of God's Spirit comes through an everyday relationship with Him.

> **To live in the light is to live intentionally. It is to walk in the bold assurance that even in the darkness of this world, God is lighting the way for us as we follow Him.**

> *Command the people of Israel to bring you pure oil of pressed olives for the light, to keep the lamps burning continually. This is the lampstand that stands in the Tabernacle, in front of the inner curtain that shields the Ark of the Covenant Aaron must keep the lamps burning in the LORD's presence all night. This is a permanent law for you, and it must be observed from generation to generation. Aaron and the priests must tend the lamps on the pure gold lampstand continually in the LORD's presence.*
> *(Leviticus 24:2-4)*

What are some things that help you stay continually plugged into God's Spirit as your source of power? (Think about people, practices, or prayers that help you feel God's presence and power in your life.)

Living in the light doesn't mean we always get it right! Instead, we lean into God as our source of power.

The same daughter who hurt herself playing flashlight tag is now a decade older. On the way to drop her off at band camp recently, we talked about her being a light for others. She shared with me that she used to think that being a light for others meant having to do everything perfectly. But she has realized that being a light means being real about her struggles and knowing God loves and forgives her. That is the hope she has to offer others. God is the light shining through her rather than her trying to never mess up!

How is God calling you to live in the light today? Sometimes that can be difficult to answer specifically. I've found that one of the best ways to shine God's light is simply to follow Him closely. And that is just what the Israelites were doing in a very literal sense.

Read Numbers 9:15-23, and describe how the people knew where and when to go:

For well over one million people in the desert, it must have been difficult to never know how long you were going to stay and where you were going. Maybe you can relate to that feeling right now. You aren't sure how long you will live in your current city and so are cautious to develop deep friendships. Perhaps you don't know how long your child will fight a disease and you just wish you knew everything would work out OK. We may not have a pillar of fire at night or a cloud during the day, but God guides us with the light of His Word and the Holy Spirit. Psalm 119:105 says, "Your word is a lamp to guide my feet / and a light for my path." Like the pillars of fire and cloud, God gave His people only the next leg of the journey without a timeline of when they would reach their final destination.

Like them, we must walk each step of our lives in faith even when we can't see much farther ahead than our next step. It can be tough to be content with just light for the next step. I often want more information about how everything will turn out. But God calls us to trust Him one step at a time. Just as the Israelites never knew whether they were staying for a day, a month, or a year at any given time, we are not guaranteed what tomorrow will bring. Yet rather than getting caught up in complaining about our lack of information, we can focus our energies on following faithfully.

What next step is the Lord calling you to make *this week* in obedience to Him? Is He calling you to stay put where you are a little longer when you are ready for a change of scenery? Is He asking you to pack up and move on when you were just feeling settled in a job, ministry, or relationship? Write a next step for right now below:

One next step that I often struggle with is taking time to rest. Whether it is my brain, emotions, or body, I have a hard time taking breaks. Productivity can be an idol in my life. There is an endless supply of things to do whether we are in a season of working a demanding job, mothering young children, or serving others during the retirement years. My mom is "retired" but she rarely sits down. From gardening, leading women's groups, playing with grandkids, making meals, and caring for my grandmother who now lives with her and my dad, she is in perpetual motion. The apple didn't fall far from the tree. Like taking a rest stop on the side of the road on a long trip, my husband and I seem to stop in life only if we are at the point of exhaustion.

God doesn't want us to wait until we can't go on anymore. He calls us to incorporate Sabbath as a regular way of life. One of the gals in the pilot group for this study mentioned that the goal of rest isn't to "produce." True rest produces nothing. I often try to sneak some productivity in my moments of rest, like reading a commentary for my writing or walking for exercise rather than leisure. But really the only thing rest should produce is relaxation and reconnection with the Lord and others.

In fact, taking time to rest isn't just a guideline God gave. We find His mandate to rest from the Creation account in Genesis to the Ten Commandments. The prophets wrote about God's serious instructions to take times of Sabbath. Jesus also mentioned our need for rest: "Jesus said to them, 'The Sabbath was made to meet the needs of people, and not people to meet the requirements of the Sabbath'" (Mark 2:27). Failing to rest can cause discontentment as we hit a wall of fatigue and burnout. This is why rest is especially important during times of preparation.

God knew that His people would need to take rest stops in the wilderness. They couldn't keep marching without taking time to rest. They had livestock, young children, and elderly among them. In Numbers 10, Yahweh instructed

Moses to make two silver trumpets to sound so the people could hear that it was time to move.

According to the Numbers 10:11-12, how long had it been since they had crossed the Red Sea?

How did they know to leave their camp in the wilderness of Sinai?

When the cloud lifted, the Israelites followed it from place to place until they came to the wilderness of Paran. They did a lot of setting up and tearing down of the Tabernacle, as well as marching division by division according to God's organizational instructions in Numbers 10:13-28. Even in the midst of all of this people-moving, God reminded them to stop and rest.

Read Numbers 10:33-36, and note what showed them where and when to stop and rest:

Remember that the ark was a physical reminder of God's provision and guidance. It included Aaron's staff, a jar of manna, and the stone tablets with the commandments (see Hebrews 9:4). The cloud was hovering over it so that the people carrying it would know where to put it down.

Read Numbers 10:36, and write below what Moses would say when the ark was set down:

As we rest, we can slow down and connect with our Creator. We can return to Him as we see Him in Creation, read His Word, gather with other believers, or just be still. God called the people of Israel to prepare by taking stock of their resources, getting organized, taking special seasons to offer themselves to God, pronouncing blessings, celebrating holy days, and doing the hard work of moving. However, He also led them to rest.

In the same way, God calls us to take a break from the work He has given us to do. He designed us, so He knows our need for sleep, recreation, and holy assembly. Yet even though the concept of stopping to rest is woven throughout the Old and New testaments, it remains difficult to incorporate into our busy lives. We go and go and go like the Energizer Bunny and then wonder why we get physically, emotionally, and mentally drained.

Where is this topic of rest hitting home with you? Take a moment to think about your resting habits.

How often do you take time to rest each week?

What are some restful activities that replenish you when you feel depleted?

Do you ever feel guilty when you rest? Sometimes I do! We need to value rest (because God does), learning to see it as an important pursuit that God instituted. In my own life, I have struggled with finding leisure activities that draw me closer to God. Media can be restful, but it shouldn't be the only option on our list of rejuvenating activities. I'm not saying that watching a movie or being online can't be part of a restful activity, but we need to put some thought and intentionality to this question:

What activities truly leave you feeling relaxed afterward? Put a check mark by any of the following activities that you would like to incorporate into your weekly routine:

__Taking a nap

__Playing a game

__Going for a walk (alone or alongside someone)

__Reading a book (not related to work)

__Reading a magazine, newspaper, or article online

__Writing letters or thank-you notes or journaling

__Painting or drawing (for fun, even if you aren't an artist)

__Baking or cooking

__Gardening

__Sitting and talking with someone

__Calling a friend or family member

Let this short list of ideas be a springboard for listing your own restful activities. Introverts like me tend to be recharged by solitary activities, while extroverts like my husband find time spent with other people restorative. I know baking wouldn't be on my list, but my friend says that's what she likes

> **When we run nonstop through life, we can stuff our emotions and issues. Rest slows us down to process and consider what really matters in life.**

to do to unwind. My husband and I have found a few comedians we really enjoy watching. Laughter can be great medicine for a weary soul!

Your ideas may look very different, but the important thing is to begin planning for rest. Put it into your schedule and guard it. Resting reconnects us to reality. When we run nonstop through life, we can stuff our emotions and issues. Rest slows us down to process and consider what really matters in life. And we all need that!

Talk with God

Spend some time in prayer, asking God to shine His light on your feet so you can see your next steps. Then carve out at least ten minutes today to do nothing but rest and let God's smile wash over you!

Weekly Wrap-Up

As we end this week, take a moment to review what we've studied. Flip back through the lessons and write something from each day that resonated with you that you can apply in your life.

Day 1: Taking Stock of Resources

_____

Day 2: Getting Organized

_____

Day 3: Special Seasons

_____

Day 4: Blessings

_____

Day 5: Lights and Rest Stops

_____

VIDEO VIEWER GUIDE: WEEK 2

Contentment Clue: **Organized**

We learn contentment as we prepare for God's blessings with organization and planning.

We learn contentment by realizing the value of the _____ God has put in our lives.

Hebrews 10:24-25 – *Let us encourage one another*

Organization with _____ leads us to greater contentment.

Numbers 2:1-2 – *The tribes were camped in an organized manner*

1 Corinthians 14:33 – *God is not a god of disorder*

In all of our _____, God reminds us that He's going to be right with us in it.

John 1:14 – *The Word tabernacled (dwelled/lived) among us*

John 6:32-35 – *Jesus is our manna, the bread of life*

In our pursuit of contentment, _____ is one of the activities we must plan for.

Numbers 10:33 – *God showed them where to stop and rest*

Week 3

CONTENT IN UNCERTAINTY

Numbers 11-14

Memory Verse

Do everything without complaining and arguing, so that no one can criticize you. Live clean, innocent lives as children of God, shining like bright lights in a world full of crooked and perverse people.

(*Philippians 2:14-15*)

DAY 1: CONTAGIOUS COMPLAINING

Do you consider yourself a complainer? I would have said "no" before delving into this study and taking notice of my thoughts and words. I've found that complaining is a universal problem. We don't like our body types, the texture of our hair, the faults of our family members and friends, our budgets, or the habits of our coworkers. Ever found thoughts like these coming to mind out of nowhere: "I wish we could afford to remodel our house. Why can't my family (or job) be more like hers? Why isn't anyone helping me in this ministry at church? She is so exclusive; I never get invited to her parties"?

Complaining is a heart attitude. Matthew 12:34b says, "Whatever is in your heart determines what you say." So, complaining words flow out of a complaining heart. We have to get to the root of the problem, which goes much deeper than just the words we say.

At the end of our study last week, we saw that the Israelites were breaking their camp in the Sinai wilderness where they had been for over a year. God had kept them in one place so that they could take a census, organize their traveling party, establish a plan for the setup and teardown of the Tabernacle, and understand God's expectations and laws for the battles ahead. Finally they are on the move. Remember from our first week of study that just three days after the people sang the song of deliverance by the Red Sea, they complained bitterly about their thirst. Unfortunately, they haven't learned much in the way of contentment. We find history repeating itself as, three days after leaving Sinai, they are at it again.

Read Numbers 11:1-3, and sum up what happened to the people according to these verses:

Complaining is a heart attitude.

Extra Insight

The word used for complain in Numbers 11:1 is a form of the Hebrew word `anan and is found in only one other place in Scripture (Lamentations 3:39). It means "(*Hithpael*) complain, murmur."[1]

Don't grumble as some of them did, and then were destroyed by the angel of death. These things happened to them as examples for us. They were written down to warn us who live at the end of the age.

(1 Corinthians 10:10-11)

Based on the Lord's reaction, it seems that complaining is a big deal to Him! The New Testament references this event in 1 Corinthians 10.

Read 1 Corinthians 10:10-11 in the margin, and note below what God wants us to learn from studying the mistakes of the Israelites in the wilderness:

These things were written to warn us. Complaining may seem like a small vice when compared to lying, adultery, or murder; but God doesn't want us to compare. He says grumbling against Him is a serious issue. Moses prayed for the people and the punishment stopped, but even then the problem continued.

Read Numbers 11:4-9 and note below who started complaining:

The term foreign "rabble" or "riffraff" sounds like a racial slur, but let's remember that Moses' own father-in-law, mentioned in chapter 10, was a Midianite. God's blessing to Abraham was that his descendants would ultimately be a blessing to the entire world. Rather than this making a statement about foreigners, it is a lesson to us about the contagious nature of complaining.

Now write below what the foreigners were complaining about:

These foreigners chose to leave Egypt with the Israelites. Perhaps they had been fellow slaves or were concerned with the unstable political landscape after the plagues. Possibly they were in awe of this God who could perform such wonders and wanted to be a part of settling in His Promised Land. No matter what their reason, they had seen God's hand of power and provision alongside their fellow travelers.

Think about what God had done for His people up to this point. List anything that comes to mind below. (If you need some reminders, look at Exodus 6:1; 13:21; 14:21-22; and 34:5-6.)

God had helped them in incredible ways, but they were saying, "God, I know you got us out of slavery, but we are not content with your provision. We don't like the food or the length of time it is taking to get us where we are going." As the foreigners among the Israelites began to crave the things of Egypt, the Israelites themselves seemed to catch the complaining bug. This might not have been the first time they started some grumbling. One commentator suggests that "because the non-Israelites would have lived at the outskirts of the camp, outside the areas designated for the twelve tribes, the fact that the Lord struck that portion at Taberah (Num. 11:1) implies that the riffraff instigated the grumbling there too."[2]

The foreigners planted seeds of discontent in those around them, which gave unspoken permission to vocalize the sin that was simmering under the surface.

I have found in my own life that sin is contagious. When I complain, I hear my kids complain. When I get angry, it can flare the tempers of those around me. When I gossip, others join in. How about you? When others are standing around the water cooler complaining about the boss, is it easier to point out your own irritations? When another woman shares her frustrations about her husband or friend, does it open the door for you to vent as well?

Recall a time in your life when your complaints have caused others to complain as well (whether family, friends, coworkers, or others):

We can set the tone in our homes, workplaces, communities, and church gatherings. Though complaining can be contagious, so can contentment! When we appreciate God's provision rather than long for something more or different, others will be impacted. Now, the last thing we want to do is put on a mask and walk around pretending everything is fine when it is not. That is not the definition of contentment. Contentment does not mean an absence of authenticity. In order to accept difficult circumstances, we must be honest about our problems; but then we must turn to God for help.

Contentment does not mean an absence of authenticity. In order to accept difficult circumstances, we must be honest about our problems; but then we must turn to God for help.

That's just what Moses did with his grumblings. The contagious complaining was like a snowball headed right in his direction; so he went to the Lord.

Read Numbers 11:10-15 and notice the emotional response Moses had to the people's lack of gratitude for what God had provided. Of all the honest questions Moses proposed to the Lord, which one stands out to you (maybe because it made you chuckle or because you could relate)?

What set Moses apart from the other complainers?

Moses took his frustrations straight to the Lord. He didn't hold anything back but even went to the point of saying, "If this is how you intend to treat me, just go ahead and kill me. Do me a favor and spare me this misery!" (Numbers 11:15). No one could accuse him of putting on a plastic smile and pretending he was content with his circumstances. The key is to bring our problems directly to the Lord and then listen for His comfort and direction.

God didn't shame Moses for having feelings. Instead, He gave him some solution-oriented steps to take.

Read Numbers 11:16-17, and write God's instructions to Moses below:

What promises did God make to Moses?

The Lord told Moses He would help him bear the burden of the people by sharing the load with seventy other leaders. He promised to come down to Moses and talk to him in the Tabernacle. God knew the weight of shepherding people, and He helped Moses with instruction and plurality of leadership. God also says He will answer us when we call on Him. Let's look at a well-known passage where we see God's shepherd's heart that leads us to follow Him with contentment.

Read Psalm 23 with fresh eyes, and write below any sections that resonate with you:

Now read these definitions of contentment put forth by Richard Swenson in his book *Contentment: The Secret to a Lasting Calm,* and underline the one that you most need to tell the Shepherd right now:

"Contentment is when we tell the Shepherd that *His provision is enough for all our physical and material needs.*"

"Contentment is when we tell the Shepherd that *His presence is sufficient for all our emotional needs.*"

"Contentment is when we tell the Shepherd that *His providence is perfect for all our future needs.*"[3]

God will provide for us, both physically and emotionally. He instructed the people of Israel to set up the Tabernacle so that they would have a tangible reminder of His presence with them. His manna fed the people supernaturally, but they complained about the lack of flavor. Both the Israelites and the foreigners craved better things instead of focusing on the miracle right in front of them. We can be tempted to do the same.

It could have been a different story. The people in the wilderness could have said,

"I don't like the boring flavor of manna, but I'm grateful God provided food so that I don't starve."

"I miss my home and traveling is difficult for my family, but I'm thankful that I'm no longer a slave and that God is guiding us with the cloud and pillar of fire."

"The future is scary and I'm not sure what battles we will face, but I choose to trust God because He said it would be a good land."

Can you think of a complaint that you have made in the last week? If so, write it below and follow it with a related blessing:

I _____,

but I'm grateful _____.

In the coming weeks, pay attention to any complaints in your thoughts or words. Every time you find yourself complaining, think or speak one blessing from God related to that complaint. Let contentment be a learned practice as you get into a regular habit of turning your posture toward God in the midst of difficult circumstances. We can't be too hard on the wandering Israelites. Most of the things we complain about are inconveniences or irritations. If I served the same meal every night in a row for a year (even if it was a family favorite), I know I would hear some bellyaching. We can't minimize the plight of the wilderness wanderers, but we *can* learn to fix our eyes on God's provision rather than our lack.

Spend a few minutes now listing some of God's blessings in your life:

> **Let's start a chain reaction of less complaining and more contentment in our homes and communities by turning to God first.**

From our reading today, we've seen that complaining is a serious matter to the Lord. He hears our grumbling and isn't pleased with it. Studying these accounts is vital so that we can heed God's warnings and not repeat the mistakes of the past. We also found that our posture is contagious. When we choose to complain, others might join in. The great news is that contentment is catchy too! Let's start a chain reaction of less complaining and more contentment in our homes and communities by turning to God first.

Talk with God

As you go to the Lord in prayer, bring all your complaints before Him as Moses did. Then listen for any solution-oriented next steps He brings to mind.

Today's Scripture Focus

Numbers 11

DAY 2: TOO MUCH OF A GOOD THING

Recently my teenage daughter asked me for something new. I told her that we wouldn't be purchasing it and that she needed to be content with what she had. Her response was, "I am content, but I just want more." I laughed with her and told her she needed to revisit the definition of contentment.

The Hebrew word often used in the Old Testament for contentment, *male´* (pronounced *maw-lay'*), is sometimes translated satisfied, fulfilled, or complete. It means "to fill, be full."[4] When we are satisfied, we aren't longing for more. Instead we are content with what we have. Charles Spurgeon, a great English preacher in the 1800s, said this: "You say, '...if I had a little more I should be very well satisfied.' You make a mistake: if you are not content with what you have you would not be satisfied if it were doubled."[5]

How would you fill in this blank?

I wish I had just a little more _____.

While we may not be whining or demanding, we often find ourselves wishing for just a little more money, time, friends, encouragement, or something else. Marketing targets us and our families, attempting to create "felt needs" within us. As consumers, the messages we receive call us to be dissatisfied with our homes, bodies, or relationships. Someone wants to sell us something that will give us "more." But getting what we think will satisfy our longings actually can have the opposite effect.

Yesterday we heard contagious complaining as the people longed for different food. Today we'll find that Spurgeon's statement about not being content with doubled blessings proved true in their lives. In fact, as they got what they wanted, it brought them a curse rather than a blessing. Sometimes getting "more" can be the worst thing for us. It can even make us sick!

Read Numbers 11:18-20 and identify what the people wanted:

God said He would give them meat for a month and they eventually would be so sick of it that they would gag on it.

Can you describe a time when you got something you really wanted but it didn't live up to your expectations?

Moses had his doubts about God's promise of an abundance of meat. Remember we are talking about one to two million people in the wilderness. He wasn't sure just how this could happen.

> **Getting what we think will satisfy our longings actually can have the opposite effect.**

Read Numbers 11:21-23 and record below Moses' concerns and the Lord's response:

Moses' concerns:

The Lord's reply:

It gives me hope that Moses, a leader who saw God do mighty miracles, had moments of questioning. He couldn't wrap his mind around how God would do what He said He would do. Moses was calculating how enough meat for everyone for a month could be possible even if they ate all their livestock and caught every fish in the sea. I can relate to Moses because sometimes I try to figure out God's promises according to my own logic.

As you think of God's promises to provide and care for you, can you describe a need in your life that doesn't seem humanly possible to figure out? (It's OK if nothing comes to mind right now.)

Now, can you think of a past experience when God met a need in a mighty way?

When we don't know how we will pay a bill, face the person who hurt us, or find any hope for a failing marriage, we must remember the Lord's character. God's response to Moses was a reminder of the power of His arm and the truth of His word. Although Moses had seen God part the Red Sea, put manna on the ground each day, and bring water from the rock, this meat challenge seemed too hard to believe.

We can see God's faithfulness and provision in our lives many times, yet when a new problem arises, we can struggle with faith. We need to revisit these truths over and over again so we don't forget. Our God is Jehovah, the self-existent One. As we read in Week 1, the prophet Jeremiah said, "O Sovereign LORD! You made the heavens and earth by your strong hand and powerful arm. Nothing is too hard for you!" (Jeremiah 32:17). If God said it, then we can take Him at His Word. He will do what He says He will do.

Now let's discover just how He brought the meat to the people.

Read Numbers 11:31-35, and describe why they named the place Kibroth-hattaavah:

Extra Insight

Scholars estimate that the amount of quail conservatively would have been more than 105 million birds.[6]

Most commentators say the literal translation of this name would be "graves of craving" or "graves of lust." The New Living translators used the term "graves of gluttony." While the exact location of this site isn't known, the concept of "more" resonates in every city across the globe. Commentator Warren Wiersbe said, "When God really wants to judge people, He lets them have their own way (Rom. 1:24, 26, 28)."[7] The psalmist wrote of these events in Psalm 106, citing the miracles seen by the wilderness wanderers and how they sang the song of deliverance after the parting of the Red Sea. Yet the people soon forgot all that God had done.

Read Psalm 106:13-15 in the margin. Besides their forgetfulness, what else do we learn about the people in these verses?

Yet how quickly they forgot what he had done!
They wouldn't wait for his counsel!
In the wilderness their desires ran wild,
testing God's patience in that dry wasteland.
So he gave them what they asked for,
but he sent a plague along with it.
(Psalm 106:13-15)

How did God respond?

The King James Version says that God "sent leanness into their soul" (v. 15). God wanted the people to realize that His provision was best. Their quest for more would not satisfy but would bring a curse along with it. They would learn this the hard way.

Like the wilderness wanderers, we can desire to be fulfilled by things that ultimately will destroy our bodies or souls. Perhaps we want a relationship so badly that we whine for it until God gives it to us, but it turns out to be more than we bargained for. Though we have freedom to make choices, not everything is beneficial for our spiritual walk. Other times our cravings for more food than our bodies need cause the plague of health problems. The desire for bigger and better can lead us to spend more money than our budget allows, leaving us with debt that feels like a weight hanging over our heads. Others of us may gorge in different areas—binge television watching, social media addictions, excess shopping, or even obsessive cleaning. We must be careful what we wish for because if we whine and complain about it, we just might get it. And it may turn out to be more of a curse than a blessing.

"The influx of quail in the biblical story is related to a natural phenomenon. Large numbers of quail migrate across the Sinai Peninsula from Africa on their way to Europe and Asia. Since these birds have relatively heavy bodies and do not fly well, they partly depend on prevailing winds to assist their flight, and they become exhausted by long journeys."[8]

The psalmist said the people of Israel:

- forgot what God had done
- wouldn't wait for His counsel
- allowed their desires to run wild
- tested God's patience

Take a moment to think through these failures of the people of Israel. Have you forgotten the good things God has done for you in the past? Write at least two good things the Lord has done in your past:

1.

2.

Often we miss God's blessings, spending our energy on our longings for more. The Israelites wouldn't wait for the Lord's counsel. When it comes to an area where you are wanting more of something, is the Lord calling you to wait? Whether it's buying a new sofa or pursuing a new career, God often calls us to wait and be content with His provision before moving ahead. Now, when God says to move, He wants us to start walking, but we better take the time to be sure in which direction He is calling us.

Is there a decision you're facing where you may need to slow down and spend some time in God's presence rather than asking for more?

God provided the Israelites with manna, but they got bored with the taste. Soon they began to develop an unclear view of the past. Rather than remembering the Egyptian slave masters and backbreaking work, they whined for meat and the onions that flavored their food. The King James Version translates Psalm 106:15 this way: "[God] gave them their request; but sent leanness into their soul." We may get the thing we beg for but find an undesired spiritual side effect coming along with it.

What are the quail in your life? Is there something you are asking God for that might not be the best for you? We don't want to camp out in the negative, but becoming aware of desires for excess can help us temper our cravings. It can be tough to say no in the moment when we desire something sweet or see the next episode in a series we're watching pop up on our screens. The abundance all around us makes access to our vices especially tempting. However, we must reflect regularly on God's provision in the past to help us accept His decisions in the present.

We also must remember that we are not helpless when it comes to bad habits and addictions we may have battled for years. Just as God's strong arm could provide meat with a strong wind, so He is able to help us in our own battles against "more."

God knows that we won't find ultimate fulfillment in anything but Him. He allowed the Israelites to experience that truth firsthand. Let's remember these things were written to warn us so that we will not experience the same plagues that can accompany any kind of gluttony. We need God to realign us to what really satisfies—a relationship with Him.

Talk with God

Spend some reflective time in prayer now. Ask God to show you any area of your life where you are not content with God's provision. Lay it at His feet and wait in His presence, asking Him to help you overcome any areas of spiritual, mental, emotional, or physical gluttony that He reveals.

DAY 3: POWER STRUGGLE

Once I was playing follow the leader with my children and some of their cousins and friends. Most of the children were between six and ten years old, but one of the little boys was four. He kept saying that he wanted to lead, so we gave him a turn; and he proudly marched to the front of the line. Quickly he became distracted by things he saw along the way—someone's dog, a stick on the ground, a nut that had fallen from a tree—and this held up the line of impatient children behind him. If he wasn't stopping for something that caught his interest, he was sauntering slowly and veering off the sidewalk because he wasn't watching where he was going. I finally said, "Sweetheart, if you want to lead, you have to stay on the path and pick up the pace."

Leadership can appear desirable, but once a person gets in position at the front of the line, they often discover it isn't as easy as it seemed. Today we will find complaining filling the ranks of Moses' fellow overseers. The difficult part was that they were his own family—his brother Aaron and his sister Miriam. They wanted the accolades of leadership but failed to stay on God's path of contentment with their positions.

> **We need God to realign us to what really satisfies— a relationship with Him.**

Today's Scripture Focus

Numbers 11 and 12

Read Numbers 12:1-3 and record two criticisms the siblings made regarding Moses:

1.

2.

First of all, they weren't happy with Moses' choice to marry a Cushite woman. Commentators have many different ideas as to the specifics regarding the matrimony. We know that Moses had married a Midianite woman named Zipporah after he fled Egypt as a young man (Exodus 2:15, 21). He took her and his sons with him when he returned to Egypt to plead for the release of his people (Exodus 4:20). At some point Moses sent Zipporah back to her father, Jethro, because, after the people crossed the Red Sea and were camped at Sinai, Jethro brought Zipporah and the children back to rejoin Moses (Exodus 18:1-2).

So, who is this Cushite woman and why are Miriam and Aaron upset about the marriage? Several explanations have been set forth by commentators (see the Extra Insight). Though we don't know the exact identity of the woman or why the harsh criticism was offered, what we do learn is the danger of being discontent with the amount of influence God has given each of us. Aaron and Miriam seemed jealous that Moses was getting most of the recognition as a leader. They claimed in Numbers 12:2, "Has the LORD spoken only through Moses? Hasn't he spoken through us too?"

It is interesting that we find both a stated reason and a hidden reason in Aaron and Miriam's complaints. Have you ever encountered this in a conflict? Understanding human nature's tendency to give one reason and still have another underlying issue equips us to ask what is really going on here. When you come up against opposition in your workplace, home, church, or community, it can be helpful to consider if a hidden reason might exist. Jesus said, "Look beneath the surface so you can judge correctly" (John 7:24).

We find in this account a great enemy to contentment: envy. Aaron and Miriam were leaders. God had called Moses from a burning bush, but he hadn't felt equipped to speak. So God had given him Aaron to help. We know from the prophet Micah, who spoke to God's people about seven hundred years after the wilderness wanderings, that God had used all three of them. Micah wrote, speaking for God, "I brought you out of Egypt / and redeemed you from slavery. / I sent Moses, Aaron, and Miriam to help you" (Micah 6:4). Miriam had also led the women in the song of deliverance after crossing the Red Sea.

It seemed that Miriam and Aaron were not content with the amount of responsibility, control, or recognition they received. Seventy leaders had just been appointed with the power to prophesy. Moses was in favor of plurality of leadership, but Miriam and Aaron didn't seem too fond of their diminishing power. Envy rots away our contentment, and the danger of it should have been fresh in all of these leaders' minds. After all, Moses had come down the mountain with Ten Commandments from God, and the last commandment had to do with desiring what others have: "You must not covet your neighbor's house. You must not covet your neighbor's wife, male or female servant, ox or donkey, or anything else that belongs to your neighbor" (Exodus 20:17). That also would include your neighbor's leadership position or popularity.

We miss God's blessings for us when we focus on our desire for what others have. Richard Swenson has said, "Envy is a one-way street to misery. It not only dishonors God, but it sets up base camp in our heads and poisons our thoughts."[9]

This accusation of Miriam and Aaron reveals what had likely been simmering under the surface for a long time: a desire for more.

As you reflect on your level of contentment, can you identify any envy simmering underneath the surface? Do you long for the vacation, home, body, ability, or amount of power that others have? Ask the Lord to identify any areas that need to be exposed and confessed before Him. Write a short prayer below, asking Him to reveal any envy that could be keeping you from a place of contentment.

Now turn back to Numbers 12:3. How does this verse describe Moses?

Moses didn't become defensive or throw a fit. Instead he allowed the Lord to intervene. We know that his position as leader wasn't his source of identity. In Numbers 11, when God gave him help in the form of seventy leaders to come alongside him, God put His Spirit on *all* of them so that they prophesied as well as Moses.

> ## We miss God's blessings for us when we focus on our desire for what others have.

Extra Insight

Read Numbers 11:26-30, and describe in a few sentences what happened:

From this account, what do you learn about Moses' character?

Moses didn't need to be large and in charge. Moses wanted what was best for God's people and celebrated when others experienced the power of His Spirit. He wasn't territorial with God's gifts. Miriam and Aaron criticized him rather than supported him in this instance. Envy will do that. It is a poison.

A peaceful heart leads to a healthy body;
jealousy is like cancer in the bones.
(Proverbs 14:30)

Read Proverbs 14:30 in the margin. What is jealousy compared to?

I hate cancer! It has claimed the lives of several people I dearly love. It spreads silently and multiplies malignant cells of destruction. Jealousy does the same. God doesn't want that for us. He longs for us to have a peaceful, contented heart.

Let's see how the Lord handled the situation on Moses' behalf.

Read Numbers 12:4-16 and answer the following questions:

Where did the Lord tell them all to go? (v. 4)

How would you summarize the Lord's message to Miriam and Aaron? (vv. 6-8)

What happened to Miriam? (v. 10)

How did Aaron respond? (vv. 10-12)

What did Moses do for his siblings who had been criticizing him? (v. 13)

How did the Lord respond? (v. 14)

Extra Insight

Part of an Old Babylonian omen text reveals that "ancient Mesopotamians also viewed a kind of skin disease as divine punishment."[11]

After taking so much grief from the complaining foreigners and Israelites, Moses now faced jealousy from his own brother and sister. God was angry and came to Moses' defense, instituting a punishment for Miriam. You may wonder why Aaron didn't receive the same consequence since he was involved in the sin. Several commentators suggest that Aaron could have been next in line, but by crying out to Moses he abated God's further wrath. While we don't know for sure, we can be sure that God isn't fond of criticism fueled by envy. He allowed Miriam's punishment to last for seven days of separation. Leprosy, like complaining, was contagious. This caused the entire traveling party to wait for her. Commentator Roy Gane points out that "a quick fix would trivialize the gravity of the situation."[12]

Miriam's sin affected those around her. In the same way, even our secret sins often manifest themselves eventually and cause others pain.

Can you think of a way that your poor choices have affected those around you? If so, describe it below:

Though we don't want to dwell in past mistakes, it's healthy to remember the consequences of our sins so that we don't repeat them. So, how can we overcome our natural tendencies toward envy and criticism? The best antidote to envy is contentment. If we are content with the amount of power, prosperity, and ability God has bestowed upon us, then we will not envy what others have. This is largely an internal posture, but the Apostle Paul says it can be learned.

The best antidote to envy is contentment.

Read Paul's words below and underline any words or phrases that stand out to you:

> *Not that I was ever in need, for I have learned how to be content with whatever I have. I know how to live on almost nothing or with everything. I have learned the secret of living in every situation, whether it is with a full stomach or empty, with plenty or little. For I can do everything through Christ, who gives me strength.*
>
> **(Philippians 4:11-13)**

The last line about being able to do everything through Christ was written in the context of contentment! Paul says it was a secret, a mystery, but he learned it. When we learn something, we must be intentional to study it, talk about it, and seek to implement it. We must name it as a goal. Marathon runners don't stumble upon the ability to run a race. They set a schedule to train. We too must mark out a path for our contentment feet. We can ask ourselves questions such as these:

- Will this decision lead me to greater contentment?
- What are my motives for wanting more _____ (cookies, houses, clothing, muscles)?
- Will I be glad I made this decision in five years?

Richard Swenson said this about contentment: "Contentment is not picked up in the natural course of living. For example, it is not acquired by simply growing older, so that at forty we are more content than at twenty."[13] This means that we must set out to learn to exercise more contentment.

Do you want to exercise greater contentment in your life? If so, write a statement of intent below:

We also must review what we are learning. I studied the Japanese language in college after spending a summer living in Japan. However, I must admit that I can only say a few phrases today. When I stopped using it regularly, I forgot what I had learned.

Similarly, Miriam had trusted God before. She wasn't godless or evil. Yet her desires went unchecked, and she found herself discontent with her role and calling. This led to consequences for her and those around her.

We can have a slow fade toward discontent in our lives that multiplies like a silent cancer when left unchecked.

Like Miriam, we can have a slow fade toward discontent in our lives that multiplies like a silent cancer when left unchecked. For this reason we must identify, evaluate, and relentlessly pursue God's plan of contentment in order to battle our fleshly tendencies toward envy.

What are some practical ways you have learned contentment in your life?

For me, I find direct parallels between my level of intimacy with God and contentment. Since contentment is a choice rather than a feeling, I am more likely to choose a contented posture when I am yielding to God's Word and Spirit on a consistent basis.

While Miriam's sin held consequences for her and the entire camp, she wasn't left behind. Likewise, God gives us grace and allows us to learn from our many mistakes so we can follow Him more closely in the future. Let's learn from the warnings we find in Numbers about criticism and jealousy and ask the Lord to help us discover the secret of contentment.

Talk with God

Confess any envy and complaining, asking the Lord to give you intentionality, spiritual discipline, and nearness to Him in order to unravel His contentment mysteries.

DAY 4: GIANTS AND GRASSHOPPERS

When I was in fifth grade, I had trouble seeing math problems on the chalkboard. My teacher sent a note home to my mom, and she took me to the eye doctor. We had to wait a week for my glasses to arrive, but I'll never forget the new perspective those spectacles gave me. On the drive home I kept commenting to my mom that I could see all the branches on the trees. She couldn't believe that I had grown accustomed to seeing blobs rather than detailed images. My glasses gave me a whole new lens for viewing the world around me. Today we will see that perspective plays a huge role in our lives.

Today's Scripture Focus

Numbers 13 and 14

Skim through Numbers 13:1-24, and record below some of the things Moses wanted the scouts to be looking for in Canaan:

Moses likely would have sent out trustworthy men. Out of one to two million people, it wasn't as though there were slim-pickings for leaders. Canaan is called the Promised Land because God had assured them He would give it to them. However, they would need to battle for it. Moses wanted his right-hand men to go in and ascertain the situation. He knew the Lord would deliver them, but on a human level he needed information to know how to pray, organize, and proceed. In the same way, God has given us His precious promises, but often we must fight battles of the mind and heart to embrace them.

What challenges are you currently facing right now? What things seem to be standing in the way of you experiencing God's peace and contentment?

Some of us are dealing with physical afflictions, relationship difficulties, time management problems, or mental and emotional battles. While we don't want to dwell on our problems, we do need to know what we are up against so that we can prepare for battle. Sometimes we don't have a specific situation but are simply battling to stay hopeful, experience peace, and learn contentment in the daily routine of life.

Where might God be calling you to pray, organize, or move forward in preparation to fight your battles? List anything that comes to mind. If you aren't sure, it's OK not to answer.

These battles often come in unexpected places. Moses knew the journey would be difficult; it had been already. Handling people on the move, food and water, and complaints had been exhausting for him. However, I'm not sure he ever expected what would happen next.

Read Numbers 13:25-33 and answer the following questions:

What were the obstacles that the ten spies reported? (vv. 28-29)

What did Caleb encourage the people to do? (v. 30)

How did the spies influence the people? (vv. 32-33)

It's tough when complaining, self-righteousness, and resistance come from those we believe to be spiritually mature. This happened to Moses when his scouts returned from the land. I think he was probably shocked to hear his best men speaking a message of fear and discouragement.

I knew parenting my daughters in the middle school years would be challenging, but I didn't expect one of my twin daughters to lose all of her hair at age twelve with an autoimmune disorder called alopecia. When my husband felt God's call to plant a church, I thought we might struggle to gather people, money, or a location for meeting. But I didn't anticipate the heartache that would come from unexpected places like relational conflicts with friends. Perhaps you didn't anticipate a divorce, depression, or the death of a loved one. I've never met anyone who said, "Life turned out just as I expected. I'm living the fairy tale." Struggle comes with the territory of living on a planet cursed with sin.

How have you seen pain come in unexpected places in your life?

Our perspective plays a huge role in how we weather unexpected difficulties. All twelve spies saw the same land, but their perspective regarding what they saw was very different. They all agreed it was a "bountiful country—a land flowing with milk and honey" (Numbers 13:27). However, ten of the spies added a big "but" to this description!

Underline the word "but" in the verse below:

> *"But the people living there are powerful, and their towns are large and fortified. We even saw giants there, the descendants of Anak!"*
>
> **(Numbers 13:28)**

Our perspective plays a huge role in how we weather unexpected difficulties.

What fear is behind this big "but"?

Only Caleb and Joshua tried to counter these reports. Often we're like the other ten spies. When it comes to us believing God's promises, we too can have a tendency to put a big "but" in our sentences: *I know God loves me,* but *I just wish I had more supportive friends (or a more understanding husband); God is all-powerful,* but *I think I might have messed everything up; God says* He will meet all my needs, but *I just don't know how we'll ever get out of debt; I want to be content,* but *nothing ever seems to go right.* Can you think of time when you have known God's truth but felt like your life had a "special situation" that required a "but" in the sentence?

The spies went in to see what they were up against in order to make plans for battle. However, the enormity of the task scared ten of them. We too can get scared when our scenarios look hopeless from a human perspective. We must be careful not to wear the glasses of fear and insecurity when we face circumstantial challenges.

The ten spies pointed out two perspectives that we can relate with all too well. Let's look at each one and then consider an alternative perspective.

The Giant Perspective

This perspective is where we focus on the problems. The situation seems gigantic, overwhelming, or too much for us to handle. When we wear these glasses, we lose faith that God is bigger and more powerful than any battle. The Israelites had seen the plagues of Egypt unfold, the Red Sea part, and the Egyptian armies drown. They ate supernatural food each day and watched water pour from a rock. Yet the giants in the land caused them to fear.

Before we shame them too harshly, let's take a look at our own lives. While we may not have witnessed the same caliber of miraculous events, we have seen God provide, protect, and walk with us through past battles. Yet with each new challenge, we too can quake in our boots when we are up against what appear to be scary giants.

On many occasions I've seen God provide for us when I wasn't sure how we would pay a bill, yet each new emergency can freak me out. God has walked our family through many health challenges, but each new problem has me battling to believe God's power and care. The giant perspective comes to us naturally, but God beckons us to see with His supernatural eyes.

The Grasshopper Perspective

While giants can trip us up, we also can be in danger of the grasshopper view. When we get our eyes set on ourselves, we only see our inadequacies and inabilities. We may believe God is powerful, but we think our past mistakes, lack of ability, or failure to get it all right disqualifies us from receiving God's blessings. Sure, God will bless and take care of those super spiritual people, but not a sinner like me. This is one of the enemy's greatest lies.

Focusing on our failures paralyzes our faith. We can agree with God about our smallness. Apart from Him we can do nothing (John 15:5). Yet He says that He has gifted us (1 Corinthians 12) and given us everything we need for life and godliness (2 Peter 1:3). With Him all things are possible (Matthew 19:26). The grasshopper perspective falls apart when we believe what God says about us rather than what we feel.

Read Numbers 14:1-4, and record below the decision that the giant and grasshopper perspectives led the people to make (see verse 4):

What emotions do you notice in the tone of these verses?

God freed the Israelites from slavery, but when the road to freedom contained some obstacles, they were ready to return to bondage. We find them protesting against God's chosen leader as an easy target for their overwhelming emotion of fear. They start stirring the pot of discontent by looking backward and "tripping" forward, saying, "If only..." (we had died in Egypt or the wilderness) and "What if" (we are killed in battle and our families are carried away as plunder). Fear can overwhelm us too when we start pitching our tents in the mental pastures of "if only" and "what if."

Recently I wrestled with God as I lay awake fretting over a situation. I would pray and meditate on God's truth, and then some new "if onlys" and "what ifs" would enter my mind. I finally cried out to God, "Lord, I trust you! Would you please give my body the memo?"

Have you ever felt this way? I don't want to minimize or oversimplify the power of fear. We all battle it to some extent. Life is scary. The Israelites faced real giants and felt like grasshoppers. Like them, we can demand that everything be easy and comfortable and freak out when we face obstacles,

Extra Insight

The spies mentioned the descendants of Anak specifically. We find descendants of these notoriously large warriors in later biblical accounts such as the giant Goliath, whom David killed (1 Samuel 17).[15]

Extra Insight

Caleb's name means "dog." Having been born a slave in Egypt, he was determined like a pit bull to follow God's commands into freedom.[16] Joshua's name was originally Hoshea, which mean's "salvation." We find in Numbers 13:16 that Moses changed his name to Joshua, which means "Jehovah is salvation."[17]

revealing we too are slaves at heart looking for easy circumstances more than we're searching for intimacy with God. We must wrestle with the Lord and pursue Him relentlessly when we face our own overwhelming situations.

Moses sets a practical example of what we can do when we feel scared. As we've seen, he dialogued with God about his insecurities regarding speaking when the burning bush voice beckoned him to lead the Israelites out of Egypt, and God told him that Aaron would help him speak. Moses also cried out to the Lord when people were complaining, and God gave him seventy leaders to help him.

Read Numbers 14:5-9 and note both the physical posture and words of the leaders to the people's cry of protest.

Physical posture of Moses and Aaron:

Words of Joshua and Caleb:

Moses and Aaron got down on the ground before the Lord. Tomorrow we will see the Lord intervene on behalf of these leaders in a huge way.

When we don't know what to do in our own scary circumstances, we can pray and ask God to transform us. We can get honest about what we are feeling and our desire to trust God. Isn't it amazing that God will help us to trust Him when we ask? In our human strength, we cannot overcome our fears. God knows we are scared, and He longs to help us. That's why the command repeated more times than any other in Scripture is, "Do not be afraid." God wants us to bring our worries to Him and then believe by faith that He is more powerful than anything we fear.

The God Perspective

Neither the giant perspective nor the grasshopper perspective has a good outcome, but there's an alternative view: the God perspective. We have the God perspective when we trust God despite our fears. We know it is possible to believe God in the midst of scary stuff. As Max Lucado has said, "Faith is the grit in the soul that puts the dare into dreams."[18]

Joshua and Caleb chose to embrace the God perspective, looking at God's power more than human weakness. They chose to view their circumstances through God's eyes, with His wisdom, and believe by faith that He would take care of them. Caleb and Joshua saw God, took Him at His Word, and wanted to do what He said.

Because our sin nature reverts automatically to the giant and grasshopper grids, we must be intentional in pursuing God's glasses. Then we can develop faith that will be the grit in our own souls to see past the natural obstacles to the supernatural possibilities.

How can you realign with God's perspective on your circumstances today? Confess below any giant or grasshopper fears that have been creeping into your thoughts and words lately:

Get rid of the habit of adding "but" to any sentence that has to do with God's power and ability in your life. Today is "no buts" day! Just as my glasses gave me a new lens on life when I was younger, let's learn from the Israelites the power of perspective so that we can align with God's view. Though at times our situations may seem gigantic and we may feel like grasshoppers, we can cling to the truth that our God is bigger than any circumstance!

Talk with God

Spend some time focusing on God's names and character qualities. Ask Him to give you His perspective on any current battles you are facing.

DAY 5: CONSEQUENCES

Watching our children reap the consequences of bad decisions isn't fun for any parent. Listen to this mom's story of heartbreak and grace.

My son was a freshman in college and decided to party regularly instead of living a God-honoring lifestyle. One night he drank way too much, was caught drinking underage with a fake ID, and evidently was belligerent with the police. He spent the night in jail and doesn't remember much of what happened. We didn't know about it for a while, but gradually he shared more and more. He had to spend his hard-earned money on bail, lawyers, and fines. The next semester he went back to school and called after a week, asking

> **Though at times our situations may seem gigantic and we may feel like grasshoppers, we can cling to the truth that our God is bigger than any circumstance!**

Today's Scripture Focus

Numbers 14

to come home. It was just too much standing up to the pressure of making bad choices. We told him that he was courageous and wise to know it wasn't the right place for him at the time. Now, a year later, he has returned to school and so far is doing well and studying hard. We pray constantly that he will let Jesus be his Lord, not just his Savior. He has experienced the consequences of legal expenses, embarrassment, physical pain, grades below his capability, and loss of his parents' trust. But he also has seen unconditional love with accountability and grace.

This mom knows the heartache of watching someone she loves experience consequences. An image used in Proverbs stands out in my mind as a picture of what happens when we make wrong choices.

Read Provers 1:29-33. What did they eat because of making bad choices and living their own way?

God says when we live our own way, we will have to eat the bitter fruit that it brings. Like the mom whose son must live with painful consequences, we often must watch those we love choke on their own schemes. It isn't pleasant.

Moses found himself in this position with the people of Israel. You'll remember that yesterday we saw they protested against their leaders and wanted to go back to Egypt. They even said in Numbers 14:2, "If only we had died . . . in the wilderness." Today we will see them "choking on their own schemes" when God shows up.

At this point, Moses and Aaron were prostrate on the ground, and Joshua and Caleb warned the people not to rebel against God by giving into fear.

Read Numbers 14:10-12 and record below the response of the people and the response of the Lord.

The whole community talked about:

The Lord said:

Moses and Aaron cried out to the Lord, and He made a grand entrance.

Think of a time when you were in a difficult situation and the Lord came to your rescue. Write a sentence or two about the circumstances below. (If nothing comes to mind right now, that's OK!)

Moses and Aaron faced the threat of big rocks being hurled their way. Maybe your stones were health problems, financial burdens, or the hurtful words and actions of others. Sometimes it can feel like the world is out to get us. We may feel that we are in the minority of those who want to follow God, but we find here that God plus us is greater than millions of stone-throwers.

Read Romans 8:31 in the margin and rewrite the last sentence of the verse in your own words:

What shall we say about such wonderful things as these? If God is for us, who can ever be against us?
(Romans 8:31)

Remember that God is for you! God didn't call the people to be perfect; He called them to believe Him. And that is what He calls us to do as well. The people disobeyed God's clear command to go in and take the land. This wasn't the unforgivable sin. We all disobey at times, and God is gracious and merciful. But when we choose our own path over His instructions, consequences will ensue. God said He would bring a plague to wipe them out and start over with Moses.

Read Numbers 14:13-16, and sum up Moses' objections to God's pronouncement of a plague:

God didn't call the people to be perfect; He called them to believe Him. And that is what He calls us to do as well.

Now continue reading Numbers 14:17-19, and write below the character qualities of God that Moses brought up when pleading on behalf of the people:

Moses defended the very people who wanted to throw stones at him! He asked God to spare them without making excuses for their complaints, threats, and unbelief. He appealed to God's reputation and character of being merciful, slow to anger, and full of unfailing love. Here we see that

God has not changed—that grace isn't only a New Testament thing. An abundance of Old Testament passages highlight God's mercy and grace. Notice the qualities of our God in these three verses so we don't lose sight of His great love while reading about His discipline toward His wayward people:

The Lord *passed in front of Moses, calling out,*

> "Yahweh! The Lord!
>   The God of compassion and mercy!
> I am slow to anger
>   and filled with unfailing love and faithfulness."
>   (Exodus 34:6)

> The Lord *is compassionate and merciful,*
>   *slow to get angry and filled with unfailing love.*
>   (Psalm 103:8)

> *Where is another God like you,*
>   *who pardons the guilt of the remnant,*
>   *overlooking the sins of his special people?*
> *You will not stay angry with your people forever,*
>   *because you delight in showing unfailing love.*
>   (Micah 7:18)

Moses asked God for grace, and he didn't argue that it was deserved. Grace is unmerited favor, and we can ask for it as well.

Is there someone in your life who needs God's grace? Take a moment now to pray for your family member, friend, neighbor, or coworker who is eating some bitter fruit right now. Ask the Lord for unfailing love, slowness to anger, forgiveness, and mercy in this person's life. If you wish, write your prayer in the margin.

Now, fill in the blanks below according to Numbers 14:20-25 to see the Lord's reply to Moses regarding the Israelites:

> I will _____ them. (v. 20)

> Not one of these people will _____.
> (vv. 22-23)

> They will not enter the land because they
> _____. (v. 22)

What were the new instructions according to verse 25?

Though our choices bring consequences, God does not refuse entrance to His Promised Land of peace and contentment based on past disobedience. God offered forgiveness and consequences simultaneously. He withheld the plague and chose to pardon them, but there were repercussions for their disobedience.

Read Numbers 14:26-38, and record a few more details that stand out to you regarding the Lord's punishment:

We see that God was very serious about their sin and that He connected the consequences to the sin. For the forty days of scouting, they would wander for forty years. They had whined that "if only they could have died in the wilderness," so He gave them what they said they wanted. They wouldn't have to worry about their children being taken away as plunder as they had feared. Their children would be the only ones to actually enter the land of promise.

This punishment may seem harsh. But what do we learn about the benefits of discipline from Hebrews 12:11 in the margin?

The Lord loves us desperately, but He calls us to follow Him. This means He is not just our Savior but also our Lord. Unfortunately, the people still didn't seem to get it. Instead of accepting God's new directions, they decided to go back and try to fix it themselves.

Read Numbers 14:39-45. How did the people try to fix the situation?

Extra Insight

One other time God determined to destroy these same people after they made a golden calf to worship, and Moses interceded for the people then too. The golden calf story in Exodus 32 and the spy story in Numbers 13–14 represent Israel's two greatest rebellions in the wilderness account.

No discipline is enjoyable while it is happening— it's painful! But afterward there will be a peaceful harvest of right living for those who are trained in this way.

(Hebrews 12:11)

God can use even our greatest failures for His glory. In the ashes of our disobedience, He can bring beauty.

"Real true faith is [our] weakness leaning on God's strength."[19]
—D. L. Moody

Extra Insight

Warren Wiersbe summed up the chapters in Numbers we've studied this week with this statement: "The entire experience at Kadesh-Barnea teaches us that there is no substitute for faith in God's promises and obedience to His commandments. Faith is simply obeying God in spite of how we feel, what we see, or what we think might happen."[20]

While I want to feel sorry for these people who had lived in slavery and now were moving through the wilderness, they sure don't make it easy. They made one bad decision after another. At first they were unwilling to go when God told them to enter the land; now they were trying to go to battle after He instructed them not to! Though we all sin at times, they seemed to habitually proceed in a direction that was the opposite of God's commands. And it led to painful punishment every time.

What connection between habitual disobedience and discontentment have you noticed in the lives of those around you?

God knows we all sin. First John 1:8 says, "If we claim we have no sin, we are only fooling ourselves and not living in the truth." Numbers 14 should not cause us to become discouraged regarding God's seeming harshness and our inability to be perfect. Instead, it should propel us to turn away from our sin and toward our holy yet merciful God.

Like the college student who made bad choices, we all have eaten some bitter fruit from living our own way. We can learn from the Israelites to stop the killer habit of disobedience and turn to the Lord in repentance. He is slow to anger, merciful, forgiving, and full of unfailing love. Though we may have consequences to bear from our choices, He will fully forgive and show us a new path to walk. God can use even our greatest failures for His glory. In the ashes of our disobedience, He can bring beauty. All we must do is break the habit of disobedience and get into the habit of choosing His way.

Talk with God

Spend some time in prayerful reflection, asking the Lord to bring to light any habitual sins where your life might be out of line with His commands. Confess and ask the Lord to mark out a path of obedience for your feet.

Weekly Wrap-Up

As we end this week, take a moment to review what we've studied. Flip back through the lessons and write something from each day that resonated with you that you can apply in your life.

Day 1: Contagious Complaining

Day 2: Too Much of a Good Thing

Day 3: Power Struggle

Day 4: Giants and Grasshoppers

Day 5: Consequences

Digging Deeper

Have you ever wondered what it would be like to be the sister of Moses? Miriam gained celebrity status but also inherited some great challenges from her position of leadership alongside him. Check out the online Digging Deeper article for Week 3, "Meet Miriam" (see AbingdonWomen .com/NumbersDigging Deeper) for a deeper look into Miriam's life.

VIDEO VIEWER GUIDE: WEEK 3

Contentment Clue: **Enough**

We learn contentment by remembering that our Savior is more than enough, even in the face of giants and fears.

Proverbs 3:25-26 – *The Lord is our security*

2 Peter 1:3 – *God has given us everything we need for life and godliness*

We can learn from the Israelites who wandered in the wilderness the

_____ of complaining.

1 Corinthians 10:1, 10-11 – *The story in Numbers is a warning to us*

Psalm 106:15 – *God sent leanness into their souls*

Complaining leads to _____.

Numbers 12:1-2 – *Moses faces harsh criticism*

Our spiritual promised lands are usually _____ with enemies that
we must overcome with God's help.

Numbers 13:25-33 — *The spies give a report*

Joshua 14:7-8 – *Caleb followed the Lord wholeheartedly*

Psalm 119:29, 123 – *Don't lie to yourself; strain your eyes to see God's rescue*

Week 4

CONTENT IN OBEDIENCE

Numbers 15-20

Memory Verse

Be thankful in all circumstances, for this is God's will for you who belong to Christ Jesus.

(1 Thessalonians 5:18)

Weekly Reading Plan

Deuteronomy 1–11

DAY 1: TANGIBLE REMINDERS

Today's Scripture Focus

Numbers 15

So far we've watched the people of Israel struggle to learn contentment through their deliverance, preparation, and uncertainty. This week as we study Numbers 15–20, we find the Lord giving them reminders about the importance of obedience and its impact on contentment. In the midst of our focus on God's holiness, we must remember to keep a balanced view. The Lord loves us. At the heart of His desire for our obedience is His great love for us. Like a loving parent longs for his or her child to refrain from destructive paths, God calls us to follow His instructions.

Throughout their journey, God gave the people detailed instructions, including the Ten Commandments. He also spoke through His servant Moses to give clear direction in specific situations. The Lord assured them of victory if they would go in and take the land; but they failed to obey, choosing instead to adopt the giant and grasshopper perspectives propagated by ten of the spies. The consequences were grave, including the death of an entire generation and forty years of wilderness wandering.

We, too, can find our promised lands occupied by enemies—such as fear, disorganization, difficult people, and uncertainty. And as the wilderness wanderers discovered, we will never find contentment by playing it safe instead of believing God. Yet like them, we can struggle to obey the Lord in the midst of daily decisions. It is my prayer that this week we'll have eyes to see through their story that contentment comes through obedience to our holy and loving God.

After the drama of the Israelites' disobedience, the people faced a journey in which they would learn to make wiser choices when it came to believing God. They knew the location of the Promised Land, but they had lessons to learn in their wandering. This reminds me of the famous line from J. R. R. Tolkien's poem in *The Lord of the Rings*: "Not all those who wander are lost."[1] The Israelites weren't lost; instead, they were learning obedience as they waited on God's timing.

Today we'll be exploring three key truths related to obedience in Numbers 15. Let's dive in.

1. Believing and looking forward to God's future promises helps us deal with present difficulties.

Obedience involves believing God's promises. After the people of Israel received their forty-year delay, God gave them many regulations and instructions for "when you enter the land." The Lord wanted them to remember that a Promised Land still awaited them. They were to keep the promise in sight, knowing that times of wandering would ultimately end and God would fulfill every promise He had made.

Read Numbers 15:1-12 and list below any foods or drinks mentioned in these instructions about grain and drink offerings:

Remember that in the wilderness the people of Israel subsisted on manna and water, which, as we've seen, they complained about. I have to wonder if their mouths were watering as they listened to the requirements for future offerings involving wine and cakes made of flour and oil. They had no grapes to press or grain to prepare while wandering through the desert. God wanted them to remember His future plans in order to endure the lack of variety in their current cuisine. They were learning patience to accept their current trials while at the same time anticipating good things ahead.

When has remembering the end result helped you push through the uncomfortable parts of a task?

Almost every time I exercise, I remind myself of my body's need for muscle tone and heart health. I also rehearse the memory of the good feeling that often comes at the end of a workout. Exercise produces endorphins in the body, giving the sensation of a natural high. These facts motivate me when I feel tired or lazy. Maybe you thought of completing a work project, working toward consistency in parenting, or meeting with a counselor to address difficult marriage issues. When we consider the end result, it helps us make wiser choices. We can ask questions such as these:

- How will I feel after I eat this?
- Will I be glad tomorrow that I made this decision?
- Next month will I look back on this as a good use of my money?
- How will the decision I make today affect my life next month, next year, five years from now?

As you reflect on your daily routines, what are some future benefits you can anticipate?

Many of the things you do have more value than you may realize. Preparing meals, organizing your home, and caring for others contribute to the future emotional, physical, and spiritual health of those you love. Working hard at your job, even if you aren't happy with your position, provides for your family. The decisions we make today will echo into the future.

The Lord reminded the very people He had just severely disciplined for their disobedience that a good future remained a part of their legacy. Their children would not be captives as they had feared. We need tangible reminders of the good things to come in order to give us perspective.

2. *While God chooses individuals and nations as His special instruments, His heart is for all the nations.*

Another key truth related to obedience in Numbers 15 has to do with sharing God's love for all people.

Skim through Numbers 15:13-31, and write a summary statement regarding God's posture toward foreigners living among the Israelites:

We saw last week that it was the foreigners who started the complaining, but God wasn't upset with them based on their ethnicity. It was their grumbling behavior that got them in trouble. While God chose the nation of Israel to be His special people, His heart has always been for the nations. Israelites and foreigners had the same opportunity to obey and present offerings to the Lord.

Read Genesis 12:2-3 in the margin. Whom did God say would be blessed through Abraham?

"I will make you into a great nation. I will bless you and make you famous, and you will be a blessing to others. I will bless those who bless you and curse those who treat you with contempt. All the families on earth will be blessed through you."
(Genesis 12:2-3)

God chose and used a people group, but His ultimate goal was to bring His message to all people everywhere. The very land He would bring His people into was situated on a trade route so that they could be a mouthpiece declaring His love and truth to the nations. When they obeyed God's laws and shared His love with others, they discovered contentment in fulfilling their purpose and calling. However, when they disobeyed and went their own stubborn way, their lives were characterized by grumbling.

Not only did God make clear His heart for the nations through His covenant with Abraham, but Jesus also began His ministry setting the nation of Israel straight regarding God's love for all people. Just after being tempted by Satan, Jesus began His ministry, teaching regularly in the synagogues. After speaking in the synagogue in his hometown of Nazareth, Jesus made a reference to foreigners in His comments about prophets not being accepted in their own country.

Read Luke 4:22-27, and write the nationalities of the following:

The widow: _____

Naaman: _____

Why is it significant that the prophets Elijah and Elisha ministered to these two foreigners? What point was Jesus making?

Here in Luke's Gospel we see that the people of Israel had lost sight of the ultimate purpose of their special calling. They got into a "holy huddle" and forgot that their contentment came from fulfilling their purpose of sharing God's love with the nations. God loves people. He sent His Son to die for "whosoever" would believe in Him (John 3:16 KJV).

Considering God's heart for all people, how can we share God's love with the nations, and how might answering that call help teach us contentment?

Just as the people of Israel were called to be close to God and to be a blessing to all people by sharing His love, we too are created for this purpose. God made us to be close to Him (Jeremiah 13:11; James 4:8) and has entrusted us with the mission of sharing His message (Matthew 28: 19-20). But as the people of Israel discovered, choosing to disobey God's call and commands never brings us peace and contentment.

My friend Bess says the most miserable time of her life was when she knew God's Word but chose to live the opposite of the truth she knew. It is the same for us. A good friend of mine has been in the process of building a house for a long time. Her husband is doing most of the work himself. Everything that could go wrong seems to have happened. From water leaks to defective flooring, it seems like the project will never be finished. We were talking about the situation, and I reminded her how the Lord wants to use this house. This home will be a ministry site that will host neighborhood gatherings, small group meetings, and youth group Bible studies, as well as the place where her own children will be discipled by their parents. I told her this house isn't about them; it is literally about the nations. Who knows what children, teens, or adults might experience God's love in that place and be called to share it with others near and far? This perspective brings us back to God's heart in our own situations as we remember that even the building of a house is truly about the nations. We can persevere and press on against all kinds of opposition when we remember God's call to share His love in all things.

> Reflect on times when you have felt close to the Lord and have shared His love with others. How would you describe your level of contentment in those times? Try to think of some tangible examples of contentment related to your thoughts, health, or emotions.

> Whether you are building a home, working a difficult job, parenting a challenging child, or frustrated in any way with your current situation, take a moment to consider how God could use you to be a blessing to others right where you are. Write some thoughts below:

We can persevere and press on against all kinds of opposition when we remember God's call to share His love in all things.

3. The Lord uses physical illustrations to help His people remember spiritual truths.

As we near the end of chapter 15, we come to a tangible reminder of the importance of obedience. The Lord wanted His people to remember who He was and why they should obey Him.

Read Numbers 15:37-41 and answer the following questions:

What did God say they should put on the hems of their garments throughout the generations to come? (v. 38)

What were they to attach them with? (v. 38)

Why did God say they needed a tangible reminder? (vv. 39-40)

How did God describe Himself? (v. 41)

Extra Insight

Most translations say the cord was blue, but the Hebrew word is *tekeleth* or *tekelet,* which means violet. This color was associated with royalty and would stand out against the white fringes just as God's commands were to stand out in the minds of His people.[2]

God knows we are prone to wander. We forget His love and care as well as His instructions for living. As new generations grow up, God's deeds of the past can seem to fade as modern ideas replace God's instructions. So, to help the children of Israel grow up remembering God's decrees, He asked them to use blue cords to attach tassels to the hems of their garments.

I've found that physical objects help me embrace spiritual truths as well. Just as the Israelites put tassels on their garments as the Lord instructed, we too can ask the Lord what He might have us do to remember His love and truth.

What are some physical reminders that have helped or that could help you not to forget spiritual concepts?

I've written Scripture verses on notecards or sticky notes and put them in places such as my bathroom, kitchen, or car to help me focus on God. Putting reminders of truth or alerts to pray in my phone, keeping special items from a women's retreat, or just seeing my Bible in my purse or on my couch have helped me think more about God.

During the pilot Contentment Project Challenge for this study, I joined several hundred women from across the country in wearing a bracelet with the word *Content* on it, moving it from one arm to the other every time we grumbled. (Several women didn't purchase the bracelet but used a hair tie or a bracelet they already owned.) Each time we moved the bracelet, we stated one of God's blessings related to our complaint. This tangible reminder helped us identify our weak areas and remember God's goodness in our lives. One mother of elementary-age children had explained to her children about her participation in the Contentment Project, and when she complained, they said, "Mom, I think you need to move your bracelet." She loved that they were learning alongside her and saw her using a physical object to grow in spiritual truth. If you are not already engaging in this practice as part of the bonus Contentment Project Challenge, I encourage you to consider trying it for seven days. (There is space at the end of the week's lessons where you can record how this exercise helped you in learning contentment.)

God knows we are weak and longs to help us remember Him. He will fulfill every promise He has made to us. God is a loving Father who has created all people to walk in relationship with Him, and He wants to help us live according to His instructions.

Which of the three key truths we've considered today stands out to you, and why?

Whichever truth most resonates with you, remember that God longs for us to know Him and grow in our obedience to Him. As we keep His Word before us, it will be alive and active in our lives!

Talk with God

Take some time to bring any questions you may have about Numbers 15 before the Lord right now. Reflect on the seriousness of sin coupled with God's longing to bless all people. Thank Him for the gift of tangible reminders of His love in your life today.

DAY 2: SIGNIFICANCE

When my friend with four young children mentioned that she couldn't find someone to watch her kids so that she and her husband could go out of town for a family event, I readily volunteered. Her kids are adorable. I see them on social media with their squishy cheeks and cute sayings. Three nights seemed like no big deal. At first it was all fun and laughter—going to the park, reading bedtime stories, and watching fun kid movies. I have to admit that by the second day, I was struggling. I had forgotten how high maintenance even the best kids can be. They need juice, snacks, and help in the bathroom.

Years had passed since my season of mothering littles, and honestly I felt thankful to get back to my routine when their parents returned. I view this mom's role as challenging but so very significant. She is providing emotional, spiritual, intellectual, and physical support and care for four human beings.

All of us grow weary in our callings at times and forget that each task God gives us has value. We tend to view what others are doing as more significant. This can lead to discontentment in our important callings from the Lord.

Today we'll find that some of the Levites who had a special role in caring for the Tabernacle resented that they were not given priestly status. They wouldn't accept their calling and desired to have more rights and responsibilities, which led to disobedience and contempt. We've seen this theme with the Israelites over and over. Many wanted to live their own way rather than yield to God's plan as presented through Moses.

Read Numbers 16:1-11 and answer the following questions:

What were Korah and the other Levites' issues with Moses? (vv. 3, 11)

How did Moses respond to them? (v. 4)

What special ministry had the Lord given Korah according to Moses? (vv. 8-9)

Who did the Levites really have an issue with? (v. 11)

Korah was able to rally 250 leaders, and he "stirred up the entire community against Moses and Aaron" (Numbers 16:19). Clearly he was a man of influence. However, instead of using his influence to encourage faith in God and support the leadership, he stirred the people toward sin.

I imagine Korah didn't set out to destroy himself and those around him. His actions possibly began with a lack of contentment with his role in the community. Maybe he didn't see the ministry of caring for the Tabernacle as enough. Granted, some of his tasks may have seemed mundane without having much glory. Perhaps he changed the oil in the lampstand or carried poles or furniture when they changed locations. He saw the people revering Moses and might have been jealous of that kind of admiration and power. This led him down a path of complaint and gossip.

We've talked about the contagious nature of sin. Leaders in particular must be careful about boldly walking down a path of intentional sin, because others will follow their lead. This is exactly what happened in Korah's case. In his pride, he dug his heels in when Moses tried to speak truth to him, and he wound up taking hundreds down with him.

> **Take a moment to consider God's call on your life right now. What are some of the daily tasks that you perform in order to serve God and others? (If you are having trouble, think of anything you do that benefits others.)**

> **Now, if *a friend* were to point out the significance of what you do for others (whether at work, home, school, or your community), what would you guess they might say? (This isn't bragging; this is realizing the significance of what God has called you to do.)**

Have you ever wished for a more visible role in which you receive more accolades or encouragement? I think if we are being honest, we've all had those thoughts and feelings. Moses tried to help Korah by reminding him of the significance of his calling. He was a Levite entrusted with the care of the Tabernacle. Remember that the Tabernacle was the physical representation of God's presence among them. Yet Korah wasn't content with his ministry.

Extra Insight

Korah was a Kohathite Levite who was a close relation of Aaron, Miriam, and Moses. Dathan, Abiram, and On were from the tribe of Reuben (Numbers 16:1). Both the Reubenites and Kohathites camped on the south side of the Tabernacle, so it's possible that their tents were close together.[3]

The 250 men who came alongside Korah were prominent leaders. One commentator observes: "This was not a rebellion of rude, impudent ruffians but of creditable leaders, esteemed men of rank. That is even more tragic, since they were not content with the privilege they had received by God's grace. Now they wanted more."[4]

Korah wanted priestly responsibilities and benefits even though God had said that only the descendants of Aaron could serve as priests. Aaron was quite old at this point, probably in his eighties. It is possible that his health was failing, because just a few chapters later we will learn of his death. Korah was fully aware of the death sentence God had pronounced on his generation after the rebellion at Kadesh (Numbers 10). Perhaps he thought that if he stepped into power and replaced Aaron, this change of leadership might reverse the pronouncement of doom and save his peers. Yet these were the Lord's instructions and the Lord's consequences. Korah could accept his role and serve, or he could rebel and lead others into disobedience. One commentator makes this point:

> The issue is gratitude versus pride. A humble, grateful person thanks God for any task and carries it out faithfully. A prideful person like Korah, selfishly desiring a bigger place, a larger slice of the action in God's kingdom, is in fact an enemy of God. Anytime one begins so heavily to emphasize "my ministry," then such a one is in danger of standing in Korah's sandals.[5]

We can relate to the allure of more. Sometimes we want more responsibility that will bring more power and prestige.

Take a moment to talk to God about your circumstances. What are three specific things you can be grateful for in relation to the responsibilities you have right now?

1.

2.

3.

Gratefulness gives us a weapon to wield against pride and envy, freeing us from comparative living.

Gratefulness gives us a weapon to wield against pride and envy, freeing us from comparative living. Appreciating your God-given role in this season of life doesn't mean you never have ambition or push yourself to do more. Contentment is not to be equated with apathy. One of the gals who participated in the contentment project shared these wise words: "Contentment does not mean you settle for less than God wants for you. Contentment is a state you reach when you are friends with God, revering and honoring Him and following His ways while living your daily life." Part of following God's ways is accepting the role He has given you and flourishing in this season. This means working at whatever you do with all your heart (Colossians 3:23) rather than wishing and whining for something different.

Write a short prayer below, asking the Lord to help you discern the difference between accepting your calling and pursuing new or different responsibilities:

Now read Numbers 16:12-14, and write below the common complaint found in these verses that we've seen throughout Numbers:

Here we see that Dathan and Abiram absolutely refused to appear before Moses—twice. They moaned about their lack of a permanent home with all the good food and drinks they desired. They looked back on slavery with rose-colored glasses, viewing their captivity years as some sort of paradise. If the people had not rebelled against Moses after the scouts returned with a bad report at Kadesh, they might have been victors living in the land of promise by now. Their disobedience brought about the consequence of prolonged wandering. However, rather than accepting their mistakes and repenting, these individuals persisted in disobedience.

It's interesting that the psalmist's account of the wilderness wanderings, which mentions only a few names regarding this rebellion, does not include Korah.

Read Psalm 106:16-18 in the margin and write below the names of the rebels named:

Again we see that envy and comparison lead to disobedience and discontent. These verses in Psalm 106 hint at what we read next in Numbers 16 regarding the consequences.

The people in the camp were jealous of Moses
and envious of Aaron,
the Lord's holy priest.
Because of this, the earth opened up;
it swallowed Dathan and buried Abiram and the other rebels.
Fire fell upon their followers;
a flame consumed the wicked.
(Psalm 106:16-18)

Skim Numbers 16:15-30, and note below the emotions, posture, or actions of Moses in the following verses:

verse 15

verse 22

verses 25-26

verse 28

What did Moses tell the people in verse 29?

It is interesting that Moses instructed those who came against him to prepare an incense censer since only the priests were typically allowed to hold them. Because Moses communicated so intimately with God and communicated His messages, he may have been repeating God's instructions. Perhaps God was revealing that they would cross any line, showing the extent of their rebellion.

Moses and Aaron were not proud, overbearing leaders abusing their power. Prideful leaders need to be confronted when they are wrong. Moses and Aaron were on their faces, humbly following God. Then Moses hurried to rescue as many as he could by telling them to get away from the tents of Korah, Dathan, and Abiram. In the midst of all this action, this verse stands out to me, as Moses says, "The Lord has sent me to do all these things that I have done—for I have not done them on my own" (16:28). Good leaders don't rely on their strength or wisdom but draw near to the Lord for guidance. In fact, Moses was so confident in the Lord that he told them they would know God had not sent him if nothing unusual happened. And with that cliffhanger, we'll end our study today and save the rest of the story for tomorrow!

We can learn from Moses to stay completely dependent on the Lord, finding our significance and taking our direction from Him. One commentator writes: "The selfish desire for greatness and authority is a common theme in Scripture. . . .And yet the most important place in the Christian life is the place of God's choice, the place He's prepared for us and prepared us to fill. The important thing isn't status but faithfulness, doing the work God wants us to do."[6]

In what area of your life do you sense God calling you to serve faithfully for now, even though at times it is difficult, mundane, or unsatisfying?

Moses couldn't be faithful to his call without God's help, and we can't either. One of the gals who participated in the pilot Contentment Project Challenge said this: "On the first day after grumbling and moving the bracelet about fifty times, I finally realized I couldn't do this by myself. I sat down in prayer, confessed my attitude, and asked God for help. After that, I was able to truly worship and concentrate on blessings." I can relate to striving in my own strength to implement godly habits. What about you?

Whether your daily duties include caring for small children, nursing a loved one through an illness, defending truth in a courtroom, working in a factory, or whatever it may be that God has given you to do, know that your role is important. By accepting God's call until He opens new doors, you will learn contentment and find that your significance comes from Him alone.

Talk with God

Take some time to bring any areas of discontent before the Lord. Ask Him to help you learn contentment by relying totally on Him for the power to see His blessings in the amazing, the awful, and the mundane.

DAY 3: LIFE AND DEATH

Although this week's passages have us reading about some harsh consequences, which can be difficult for us to swallow, they remind us that we serve a holy God who longs for us to obey His instructions. Learning contentment in obedience is our theme this week, but let's not forget that the God we are called to obey is a good, good Father. He loves us and has provided the sacrificial offering of His only Son to cleanse us from sin. We don't learn to obey an unpredictable tyrant but the loving and faithful God who created us. Today we'll find two tangible reminders for the people of Israel. One would jog their memory of the death that results from disobedience, and the other would represent the life-giving power of God's holy presence.

Yesterday we left the nation hanging on Moses' statement, "If nothing unusual happens, then the LORD has not sent me" (Numbers 16:29). Let's pick up the story in the next verses.

Read Numbers 16:30-35 and answer the following questions:

What did Moses say would be evidence that the leaders had shown contempt for the Lord?

> By accepting God's call until He opens new doors, you will learn contentment and find that your significance comes from Him alone.

Today's Scripture Focus

Numbers 16 and 17

Digging Deeper

We know that God hasn't changed, but how do we reconcile what appears to be harsh responses to sin in the Old Testament with the grace shown by Christ toward repentant sinners in the New Testament? For more insight into God's shepherding of a nation (OT) and His church (NT), see the online Digging Deeper article for Week 4, "Shadows" (see AbingdonWomen .com/NumbersDigging Deeper).

What happened?

Yikes! The God who had powerfully delivered His people from slavery also used His might to discipline those who opposed Moses and Aaron. Now, while we serve this same God and His character has not changed, we must acknowledge that the needs of a nation that lived under the old covenant, required a governing system, and had one God-appointed leader are quite different from those of the body of Christ that lives under the new covenant, with Christ Himself as its head (see the Digging Deeper article for Week 3 for more on this).

We learn from Numbers 26:11 that the sons of Korah did not die, so we can conclude that they must have chosen not to stand with their father in his rebellion. His descendants later became temple singers who wrote a number of the psalms. This gives me hope in the midst of all this despair! Some have called the forty years of wandering the longest funeral march in history. God said the entire generation would die before the people of Israel would enter the Promised Land, and many of them fulfilled this pronouncement in these five verses!

The Lord then gave the people a physical reminder of an important truth.

Tangible Reminder #1: Disobedience Leads to Death

We see from this first physical reminder that Moses did not rely on his own own wisdom but took his directives from God.

Read Numbers 16:36-40 and fill in the blanks below according to the text:

_____ told Moses to have Eleazar pull all the incense burners from the fire. (v. 36)

The incense burners were to serve as a _____ to the people of Israel. (v. 38)

The bronze was to be hammered into a thin sheet to overlay the _____. (vv. 38-39)

This physical illustration is cold, metallic, and lifeless, reminding the people of the death that comes from disobedience. While the ground will not open up and swallow us when we make a wrong decision, we must remember that living contrary to God's instructions leads to the death of relationships, emotional health, and intimacy with the Lord. We will explore why we don't see this kind of judgment in the New Testament or today a little later in our study.

Recall a time in your life when disobedience to God's commands brought pain into your life:

Being scared of God wasn't enough to transform the people's hearts (and it still isn't today). Right after the devastating display of God's power, the people had not softened through fear. We read, "The very next morning the whole community of Israel began muttering again against Moses and Aaron, saying 'You have killed the Lord's people'" (Numbers 16:41). The people were scared, but not with a reverence that led to obedience. After the people muttered again, God sent a plague that killed 14,700 people. Many more would have died if Moses hadn't interceded and instructed Aaron to purify the people with an incense burner (Numbers 16:45-49).

These judgments partially fulfilled God's promise that this whole generation would not live to see the land of promise. We must keep in mind the context of the old covenant that was characterized by the law. While Jesus did not abolish the moral and ethical laws given to Moses but fulfilled them, He taught that obedience must be from the heart rather than merely technical observance of the letter of the commands (Matthew 5:17).

Jesus did not hold to strict Old Testament laws regarding hand washing (Matthew 15:1-2), Sabbath restrictions (Matthew 12:1-14), and dietary laws (Mark 7:1-23). In addition, the death of Jesus fulfilled the laws regarding animal sacrifice and ceremonial laws.

> *"Don't misunderstand why I have come. I did not come to abolish the law of Moses or the writings of the prophets. No, I came to accomplish their purpose."*
>
> *(Matthew 5:17)*

Old Covenant or New Covenant?

Read each passage and mark the statements that follow as referring to the old covenant (OC) or the new covenant (NC):

Jeremiah 31:31-34

1. ___OC & NC___   This covenant will not be like the one I made with the people I brought out of Egypt.

2. _____   I will put my instructions deep within them and I will be their God and they will be my people.

3. _____ I will forgive their wickedness and remember their sins no more.

Romans 7:4-12

4. _____ The law aroused evil desires and produced sinful deeds.

5. _____ You are united with Christ who was raised from the dead and released from the power of the law.

6. _____ We serve God now in the new way of living in the Spirit.

7. __OC & NC__ The law itself is holy and its commands are right and good.

2 Corinthians 3:4-11

8. _____ This covenant included written laws and ends in death.

9. _____ This covenant is of the Spirit and gives life.

10. _____ This covenant began with such glory that the people of Israel could not bear to look at Moses' face glowing with brightness.

11. _____ This covenant is more glorious and remains forever.

Galatians 2:16-20

12. _____ This old system of law has already been torn down.

13. _____ We stop trying to obey all the requirements of the law under this covenant.

14. _____ Under this covenant we live crucified with Christ so that He gives us the power to live new lives.

Hebrews 8:13

15. _____ This covenant is obsolete and will soon disappear.

Answers: 1. OC & NC 2. NC 3. NC 4. OC 5. NC 6. NC 7. OC & NC 8. OC 9. NC 10. OC 11. NC 12. OC 13. NC 14. NC 15. OC

Based on what we find in these Scriptures, we are no longer under the penalty of the law because of Christ's death on the cross, which brings us forgiveness of sin. Though we are no longer required to observe all of the laws expected of the nation of Israel—such as dietary laws, Sabbath regulations, and mandates that were given for particular people and seasons—we still look to the Old Testament teachings for wisdom and guidance in how to live a holy life. As 2 Timothy 3:16 reminds us, all Scripture is inspired by God and useful for teaching and training in right living. Freedom from the Old Testament law does not give us license to relax our moral standards. Jesus actually raised the bar on Old Testament teaching, pointing to heart motives over behavior modification (see Matthew 5:20-28). As we've seen, He said Himself that He didn't come to abolish the law but to fulfill it. Following His example and teaching, His disciples taught believers to live in obedience to God through the power of Christ, because this leads to life (Romans 1:5; Philippians 2:12).

Tangible Reminder #2: Obedience Leads to Life

As we move on to the next physical illustration God gave His people, found in Numbers 17, we'll find it greatly contrasts the bronze altar cover that was lifeless and cold.

Read Numbers 17:1-11, and either draw or describe what Aaron's staff looked like according to verse 8:

God wanted to settle this issue of leadership once and for all. So in addition to the physical reminder of the death that results from disobedience, He used an illustration of blossoming life and nourishment to remind His people that obedience leads to life.

We know for certain that God wants us to choose life. In Deuteronomy we find these words to the new generation who were about to enter the land:

"Today I have given you the choice between life and death, between blessings and curses. Now I call on heaven and earth to witness the choice you make. Oh, that you would choose life, so that you and your descendants might live!

Extra Insight

Because the New Testament was not complete when the Apostle Paul wrote his second letter to Timothy, 2 Timothy 3:16 is likely referencing the Old Testament as well as the Gospels.

Extra Insight

Aaron's staff budded and produced almonds, which could be symbolic of watchfulness. "The Hebrew word for 'almond' is derived from *šqd*, and the verb *šqd* means 'watch/be awake.' The connection is that the almond tree blossoms in the spring before other trees."[7]

Extra Insight

Jude mentioned Korah as an example of rebellion alongside Cain and Balaam in his warning to the early church regarding false teachers (see Jude 11).

*You can make this choice by loving the L*ORD *your God, obeying him, and committing yourself firmly to him. This is the key to your life. And if you love and obey the L*ORD*, you will live long in the land the L*ORD *swore to give your ancestors Abraham, Isaac, and Jacob."*

(Deuteronomy 30:19-20)

While we may struggle with the harsh consequences we've discovered in these passages, may we never forget that God's way leads to life and peace; and He desires for all of us to choose life!

Consider how following God has led to life and peace for you. Write below any specific examples that come to mind:

When we yield to God's way we find contentment sprouting and blossoming in our lives, bearing fruit that impacts those around us.

Even after the Lord caused Aaron's rod to sprout and blossom, the people chose to dwell in despair. They claimed that they were ruined and that everyone who came close to the Tabernacle was doomed to die (Numbers 17:12-13). They exaggerated and focused on gloom and doom rather than on loving God. No amount of negative or positive reinforcement shook their defeatist worldview.

How about you? Are you allowing past bad choices or current disobedience to cloud your understanding of God's love and grace? Through the bronze altar cover and the sprouting rod, our God reminds us that disobedience leads to death but following Him leads to life. While we cannot fully understand the ways of our mysterious God, we can thank Him for our Savior Jesus Christ who fulfills the law. When we yield to God's way we find contentment sprouting and blossoming in our lives, bearing fruit that impacts those around us.

Talk with God

Bring all your thoughts and questions before the Lord today. As I have studied the Book of Numbers, I have been praying Psalm 119:18: "Open my eyes to see / the wonderful truths in your instructions." Join me in this prayer today and throughout the remainder of our study as we continue to seek God's truth for our lives today from the story of God's people in the wilderness.

DAY 4: PURIFIED

As we're digging into the Book of Numbers, we're encountering some passages that might be perplexing or unfamiliar to us. Who can say that God's Word is boring, right? Today is no exception as we explore some topics that might seem odd or foreign to us. I can't remember the last time I heard a sermon on priestly duties, ritual cleansings, or a red heifer. You may be saying to yourself, "Did she just mention a red cow?" Yes, I did! Hang in there with me today because we don't want to miss God's message to us in His Word, which is alive and active.

By looking at these obscure practices of the wilderness wanderers, our goals are to:

1. Gain a general knowledge about the practices of this period so that the whole of Scripture makes more sense.
2. Understand the priestly duties a little better so that we can make connections to Jesus as our own high priest, who mediates our relationship with God the Father.
3. Learn how God used certain practices to remind the people of important, timeless truths about life and death and sin and forgiveness.

Let's get started!

Read Numbers 18, and write below any phrases, insights, or questions that stand out to you:

Here are some things I noticed that I'd like to highlight:

- The Lord spoke directly to Aaron rather than Moses this time (18:1). This is the man who helped fashion a golden calf as an idol (Exodus 32) and joined his sister Miriam in rebellion against Moses (Numbers 12). It reminds me that God speaks to humble, repentant followers, not just perfect people.

- God asked the people to give their first fruits, the best of everything they had. Our offerings to God shouldn't be our leftovers (18:12-13).
- The principle of "redemption as payment" was made for the firstborn sons and animals to redeem them (18:15-17). Christ paid for our sins and redeemed us!
- Though the Levites would have no land of their own, God said He would be their inheritance and allotment (18:20). Serving God may not always bring physical wealth, but God offers us the spiritual riches of a close relationship with Him.
- The Lord made distinctions about what was holy and what was common (18:32). While God wants us to draw near and calls us friend, we must not forget that He is set apart as holy.

As you consider these concepts, as well as the things that stood out to you, in what ways do they resonate in your own life? Write below any areas where you feel convicted or encouraged or where you have already received some direction from the Lord through this chapter:

While no verses from Numbers 18 may be underlined in your Bible or on your list for memory work, we know that *all* Scripture is inspired by God (2 Timothy 3:16). It helps us grow a bigger view of God and His sovereign plan over the course of history.

Now read Numbers 19, and answer the following questions. I pray that as you read these verses you'll not only see a red cow and some weird rules but also a fuller picture of Christ and His sacrifice.

How is the red heifer described? (v. 2)

What was to be done with the heifer? (vv. 3-6)

Why does the text say this ceremony was performed? (v. 9)

A heifer is a young female cow that has not produced her first calf. A person who came in contact with the dead was considered "unclean" or unable to approach God because death is the final result of sin. This is why a special sacrifice had to be made to cleanse (symbolically, not literally) a person who came in contact with death. Some have suggested that God wanted the Israelites to stay away from dead bodies because of the risk of disease or bacteria, but most commentators agree that the ritual was symbolic rather than medical.

Do any of the characteristics of this red heifer scenario remind you of Christ? If so, list them below.

Let's consider some similarities together. First of all, the heifer was to be perfect, without defect. We know from Scripture that Christ never sinned (2 Corinthians 5:21; 1 Peter 2:22). The red heifer is the only time we find a specific mention of a color requirement for an animal. In the standard sacrifices found in Leviticus 1–9, the animals had to be perfect but not red. So this color distinction sets this sacrifice apart from the others. Some other differences from the standard sacrifice in the red heifer treatment include that the animal was female, slaughtered outside the camp rather than sacrificed at the altar, and burned in its entirety with no priestly identification or draining of blood. We see here some differences and some similarities to Christ. Christ was not a female, and His body was not burned. However, His sacrificial offering for sin was made outside the city rather than on an altar.

The cedar, hyssop, and scarlet thread were "elements...associated in the Hebrew mind with cleansing properties (see Leviticus 14:4)."[8] The ashes of the red heifer were mixed with water for cleansing. In this portrait we see a foreshadowing of Christ in the New Testament as a purifying agent in our lives. So our parallels between Christ and the red heifer include:

- perfection
- a sacrifice not made on the altar
- cleansing properties to purify uncleanness

Foreshadowings aren't exact but provide an image like a shadow shows the outline of a person or thing. The red heifer gave a glimpse of God's future plan to offer His Son to make us clean.

Now read the passage from Hebrews below. Underline any mention of the priests and the Tabernacle; circle any mention of the blood and the ashes of the heifer:

> 11Christ has now become the High Priest over all the good things that have come. He has entered that greater, more perfect Tabernacle in heaven, which was not made by human hands and is not part of this created world. 12With his own blood—not the blood of goats and calves—he entered the Most Holy Place once for all time and secured our redemption forever.
>
> 13Under the old system, the blood of goats and bulls and the ashes of a heifer could cleanse people's bodies from ceremonial impurity. 14Just think how much more the blood of Christ will purify our consciences from sinful deeds so that we can worship the living God. For by the power of the eternal Spirit, Christ offered himself to God as a perfect sacrifice for our sins. 15That is why he is the one who mediates a new covenant between God and people, so that all who are called can receive the eternal inheritance God has promised them. For Christ died to set them free from the penalty of the sins they had committed under that first covenant.
>
> (Hebrews 9:11-15)

According to these verses, what has Christ accomplished for us?

How is this good news for you personally?

If we have nothing else to be content about today, we can express thankfulness for the blood of Christ that removes the stain of our sin!

Old Testament believers were ceremonially cleansed in accordance with their obedience to the laws we see in Numbers. It wasn't the actual rituals but the heart of obedience behind them that made them acceptable. The Lord still longs for us to have a heart of obedience to Him.

While we no longer operate under the Tabernacle system, with priests representing us before the Lord, we see glimpses of Jesus in their ministry. We notice God's unchanging character in redemption and caring for His servants. The red heifer provided a shadow of what Christ would ultimately accomplish. He provided for our cleansing when He died on the cross. If we have nothing else to be content about today, we can express thankfulness for the blood of Christ that removes the stain of our sin!

In these chapters focused on obedience, I hope you didn't miss God's desire to cleanse us. As it says in Hebrews 9:14, through Christ our consciences are purified from sinful deeds so that we can worship God. Let's end our time today worshiping God, knowing that our sin does not define us. He longs for us to obey; but even when we veer off course, God has made a way through the blood of Christ to cleanse us from all unrighteousness!

Talk with God

Write a prayer in the margin thanking Christ that we can have purification from sin because of His sacrifice. Celebrate the freedom from sin that the gospel affords you today.

DAY 5: ARGUING

Today's Scripture Focus

Numbers 20

I had an argument with one of my daughters last night about the shared use of the bathroom among my three teenage girls. She wanted me to demand that her sister get out of the tub so she could take a bath. I told her that it was late and she needed to take a shower in the other bathroom. She argued that her sister was purposely taking a long time just to annoy her. She just about lost her mind—over a bath.

Some of you are remembering childhood arguments with friends or siblings, or perhaps you have children who argue over senseless things as well. We can laugh about silly disagreements, but it really isn't funny when a person under your care and authority continually argues against you. Even if the context of the argument is minutia, it can wear you out! It's difficult to embrace contentment in the throes of an argument.

I can find myself in my daughter's shoes with others over the silliest things. An argumentative spirit comes out in me when I have to wait longer than I think I should or I don't get my own way. How about you?

What types of situations tend to bring out your argumentative nature?

Whether it is seeing injustice, having wars with words, or simply not getting what you want, we can all find ourselves arguing at times. Today we will find the Israelites putting up a fight.

Read Numbers 20:1-6 and answer the following questions:

What personal loss was Moses experiencing? (v. 1)

What were the people blaming Moses for? (vv. 3-4)

How did Moses respond physically? (v. 6)

Here we find the same old people saying the same old things. The people of Israel were wishing they had died in the plague that took out over 14,000 people! Again they were focused on greener grass—even if that grass was dead! They missed the grain, figs, grapes, and pomegranates from their days of slavery. When we find ourselves obsessing over someone else's greener grass, it's usually time to water our own spiritual yards. Speaking of water, we must acknowledge that it is truly a need rather than a want. We can't survive without it. Yet instead of humbly asking the Lord for water, the Israelites argued and complained.

We too struggle with desires for better—better food, homes, clothes, or cars. How about better jobs, family members, churches, or friends? But we also have basic needs. Not only do we need water; God created us with a need for relationships, security, and love. When we aren't getting what we want or need, we can either take a posture of prayer and humility as Moses and Aaron did, or we can choose to blame and argue.

Many times over the course of each day, we will face the decision of contentment. Will we come to God when we feel we lack something, or will we complain? Now this doesn't mean there is never a time to authentically share your pain with others. Moses poured out his heart to God in an argumentative way in Numbers 11. We see throughout Scripture, particularly in the psalms, that God welcomes us to bring our complaints to Him. However, from this account in Numbers we find a caution against continually arguing against God's instructions and provision. We all know the difference between sharing with a close companion and scoffing from afar.

How have you been doing lately? As we are now more than halfway through our study in the Book of Numbers, think about how you have grown in learning contentment. If you are struggling to notice any measurable changes in your life, remember that character and spiritual changes often happen under the radar. Consider your thought life, the health of close relationships, or the change of tone in your prayers or attitude. Notice how God is at work, and ask Him to help you embrace what He has provided for you.

> Stop now and think about any of your own "grain, figs, grapes, and pomegranates" from the past that you are complaining about—things you used to have and enjoy or things you don't have but want. Write a brief prayer below releasing these *desires* to the Lord and presenting requests for any true *needs* that you have right now:

> Turn back to the text and continue reading Numbers 20:7-13. Then answer the following questions:

> What was God's specific command to Moses and Aaron? (v. 8)

> What did Moses actually do? (v. 11)

> What was God's response? (vv. 12-13)

> Does this punishment seem a little harsh to you? Why or why not?

I think we are seeing a glimpse of a fuller picture of Moses' attitude. He was fed up with the people! He went through the motions of seeking God, but in the end he did not fully obey God's command. I want to think up a lot of excuses for him: "God, Moses had just buried his sister, Miriam, so he was grieving. He had to deal with these complaining people who were so ungrateful. He was tired of being blamed continually. Was it such a big deal that this one time he did it his way instead of Yours?" Is anybody with me here?

Yet throughout this week we've seen that our God is gracious but also holy. He wants us to listen and obey. It's so easy to excuse our lack of complete obedience, but as we scour the pages of Scripture we see that those individuals God used to do mighty things for His kingdom were sold-out for Him (Noah, Abraham, Joshua, Deborah, Esther, David, Isaiah, Mary, Peter, Paul).

Don't we all want to be close to the Lord and used of Him? This means being faithful in the large and the small. Jesus said, "If you are faithful in little things, you will be faithful in large ones. But if you are dishonest in little things, you won't be honest with greater responsibilities" (Luke 16:10). Moses was called to be faithful even in the smallest difference between speaking to the rock and striking it.

Ask the Holy Spirit to help you identify any area of incomplete obedience in your life right now. Write a prayer below expressing your intent to fully obey:

Now brainstorm anything that might help you embrace complete obedience in this area:

If you couldn't think of anything, consider these ideas:

- Is there someone you need to tell about your commitment for accountability?
- Is there a tangible reminder you can put in your home, car, or purse that you will see and be reminded to be faithful?
- Is there something you need to get rid of to remove temptation?

It may be a small thing such as eating food that isn't a healthy choice for your body or a bigger thing such as forgiving someone who has hurt you. We must search the Scriptures and wrestle with God in prayer to know with certainty what God is asking us to be faithful in doing. We shouldn't feel guilt or shame—that isn't God's voice. Instead, we sense loving conviction to make changes that will lead to freedom.

The Lord renamed the place where the people complained Meribah, which means "arguing." We don't want to live in Meribah. If you've been camped out there, run fast toward the path of obedience!

Talk with God

Spend some time with the Lord thanking Him for the access and forgiveness you have through Christ. Also ask God to continually show you any areas where your discontent might be rooted in some sort of disobedience.

Weekly Wrap-Up

As we end this week, take a moment to review what we've studied. Flip back through the lessons and write something from each day that resonated with you that you can apply in your life.

Day 1: Tangible Reminders

_____

Day 2: Significance

_____

Day 3: Life and Death

_____

Day 4: Purified

_____

Day 5: Arguing

_____

If you wore a bracelet this week as a tangible reminder to practice contentment, record in the margin what you learned from the experience.

> We must search the Scriptures and wrestle with God in prayer to know with certainty what God is asking us to be faithful in doing.

VIDEO VIEWER GUIDE: WEEK 4

Contentment Clue: **Grateful**

We learn contentment by counting our blessings.

The Lord gives physical reminders to _____ His people remember to obey.

Numbers 15:37-41 — *Tassels on clothing*

The Lord calls us to freedom from _____ living.

Numbers 16:1-3 — *Korah's rebellion*

1 Thessalonians 5:18 — *Be thankful in all circumstances*

Colossians 3:23 — *Work willingly as for the Lord*

Partial or slow obedience is still _____.

Numbers 20:8, 11 — *Moses struck the rock twice*

Week 5

CONTENT IN OPPOSITION

Numbers 21-26

Memory Verse

Let's not get tired of doing what is good. At just the right time we will reap a harvest of blessing if we don't give up.

(Galatians 6:9)

DAY 1: OCCUPIED TERRITORY

Weekly Reading Plan

Deuteronomy 12–24

Today's Scripture Focus

Numbers 21

Right now my husband, Sean, and I feel like we are in a battle. He woke up at four this morning and couldn't go back to sleep, so he wrestled in prayer about what to do in a situation with our teenage daughter. We want to honor God and protect our daughter, and we know she isn't going to be happy with a decision we feel led to make concerning her. I know God has a great future ahead for our family, but many times it feels like we must battle to get there.

The expectation that our obedience will deliver us from all struggles, with God immediately ushering us into a land of blessing, is one of the greatest misconceptions we can have regarding the life of faith. Most often our promised lands are already occupied, and we must battle to enter into the peace, rest, and abundance God has promised.

In what ways have you faced opposition or trials in your journey with the Lord? List some recent setbacks and/or older stories.

I wish the land flowing with milk and honey was always vacant and easy to occupy, but in the Scriptures we find a recurrent theme of God calling us to overcome opposition, relying on His help and strength. As we dig into Numbers 21 today, we'll find three physical illlustrations that connect to the New Testament revelation of Christ. Let's explore each one together.

1. Manna

As chapter 21 opens, we learn that the Canaanite king of Arad attacked Israel, and the people made a vow to obey the Lord. With God's help, they defeated their enemy. However, after God's incredible deliverance, the people reverted to old habits.

> The expectation that our obedience will deliver us from all struggles, with God immediately ushering us into a land of blessing, is one of the greatest misconceptions we can have regarding the life of faith.

Read Numbers 21:1-5. What two specific complaints did they make? (vv. 4-5)

1.

2.

As the people made their way around the land of Edom, they became impatient on the journey and bored with the food. Here we find a key contentment killer: *impatience*.

We don't like to wait. Many of the women who participated in the pilot Contentment Project Challenge talked about becoming impatient when faced with traffic, long lines, and delayed appointments. When things aren't moving at the pace we expect, we can find ourselves complaining.

When have you needed patience while waiting for something (it could be something major such as a job promotion or something minor such as a grocery store line)?

Currently I am waiting for hearts to soften in some relationships. Sometimes it feels that change will never come. I've also needed patience during long family car trips and pregnancy. I was eight days overdue with my son, and it felt like my situation was endless! I stomped around our apartment bemoaning a seemingly never-ending pregnancy.

In order to learn contentment in the midst of opposition or difficulty, we must allow God to grow patience in us through the Holy Spirit. The Israelites not only complained about the length of the journey, but they also grumbled about the food God supernaturally provided.

He rained down manna for them to eat;
he gave them bread from heaven.
They ate the food of angels!
God gave them all they could hold.
(Psalm 78:24-25)

Look again at Numbers 21:5. What adjective did the people use to describe the food?

Now read Psalm 78:24-25 in the margin. How does the psalmist describe the manna?

God provided the food of angels, bread from heaven; but in their discontent they reimagined it as miserable or horrible. When the Israelites first named it manna, they said it tasted like honey wafers (Exodus 16:31), so we know they didn't originally think it was so bad. This food they loathed meant much more than their daily sustenance.

Read John 6:32-35 and answer the following:

How many times do you find the word *bread* in this passage?

Who is the true bread from heaven?

How did Jesus refer to Himself in verse 35?

"I am the bread of _____."

This bread in the wilderness typified how God longs to provide for us. As food sustains our physical bodies, so Christ is the daily nourishment needed by every person. He alone can satisfy the God-shaped hole inside of us. And He is the source—the provider—of all that we need.

Write below one way that God has satisfied your needs as the bread of life. Consider ways He has met your hunger for relationship, truth, wisdom, direction, or material necessities.

2. The Bronze Serpent

Right after the Lord delivered the wilderness wanderers from attacking armies, they began to complain. And God responded with correction. God's discipline often seems to come on the heels of our grumbling.

Read Numbers 21:6-9 and write a summary of the punishment and the remedy found in this passage:

Punishment:

Remedy:

Isn't it fascinating that the very thing biting at the feet of the wilderness wanderers was used as the object the people should gaze upon in order to be healed? Imagine snakes at your feet for a moment. I could have a panic attack just thinking about it. Yet Moses called the people to get their eyes off the enemies biting at their legs and gaze instead at the bronze serpent he lifted up. It would require great faith to stop swatting at the snakes below and lift their eyes up to that pole!

This obscure story of the bronze serpent has some incredible correlations with Christ. In fact, a New Testament allusion to the bronze serpent is found near one of the most famous verses about Christ in all of Scripture, John 3:16—words that were spoken by Jesus Himself.

Read John 3:14-17 in the margin, and write below any similarities you discover between Christ and the bronze serpent:

"As Moses lifted up the bronze snake on a pole in the wilderness, so the Son of Man must be lifted up, so that everyone who believes in him will have eternal life.

"For this is how God loved the world: He gave his one and only Son, so that everyone who believes in him will not perish but have eternal life. God sent his Son into the world not to judge the world, but to save the world through him."

(John 3:14-17)

Just as the bronze serpent on the pole was a remedy to the very thing infecting the people, so Jesus on the cross became the answer for the sin that infects us: "God made Christ, who never sinned, to be the offering for our sin, so that we could be made right with God through Christ" (2 Corinthians 5:21). God calls us to turn from the sin "nipping at our heels" and gaze at Christ. While the Israelites were physically saved by looking up at the bronze serpent, we look up at Christ for spiritual life.

Consider also the personal nature of the decision to look up. Each Israelite had to choose to look at the bronze serpent. In the same way, Jesus calls each of us to look at Him when sin threatens to devour us. It isn't a group plan; we must make the decision individually to trust in Him for salvation.

The impatience and complaining of the Israelites provoked God's judgment. Their sin brought consequences, leading to death. As Romans 6:23 tells us, sin leads to death in our lives as well. Yet the good news is that God's heart is to save us, as it always has been! In the wilderness He used a bronze serpent as a foreshadowing of His plan for ultimate salvation. Christ's sacrificial death on the cross was God's means of satisfying the judgment of sin to save us from spiritual death. As we read in John 3:17, He didn't come to condemn the world but to save it!

Because of the cross, we are free from the penalty of sin; but we still battle daily the power of sin in our lives. The flesh wars against the spirit, and our disobedience brings real consequences in our lives.

Impatience can cause us to make ungodly decisions.

Complaining can sour our view of things.

Prayerlessness can lead to worry and fear.

These are just a few examples of the sin that bites at our feet and threatens to trip us up. And the solution for both the power of sin in our lives and the penalty of that sin is Christ!

So, the next time sin bites at your feet, choose to turn your eyes upon Jesus. None of us can fix our sin problem by swatting at bad habits or temptations. Instead we must come to God in humility and admit that our way isn't working. We must fix our eyes on Christ and ask Him to transform us, rather than try to manage our sin on our own.

Write a prayer below thanking Jesus that He was lifted up on your behalf and asking for His help with any impatience or complaining in your life:

> **We must fix our eyes on Christ and ask Him to transform us, rather than try to manage our sin on our own.**

3. Water

After the manna and bronze snake, we come to a third physical substance in Numbers 21 that connects with the New Testament revelation of Christ.

Read Numbers 21:10-20, and identify what the Israelites wrote a song about:

God provided water, and the people worshiped and sang. This is the first song we've seen the people sing since the Red Sea deliverance in Exodus 15. Here we find some hope for this new generation. They praised God for water *without* whining and complaining for it impatiently! Water represents life, giving us another visual reminder of God.

According to John 7:37b-39 in the margin, who is our living water?

> *"Anyone who is thirsty may come to me! Anyone who believes in me may come and drink! For the Scriptures declare, 'Rivers of living water will flow from his heart.'" (When he said "living water," he was speaking of the Spirit, who would be given to everyone believing in him. But the Spirit had not yet been given, because Jesus had not yet entered into his glory.)*
>
> *(John 7:37b-39)*

The Holy Spirit is living water for our souls. We long for Him to "Spring up, O well!" in our souls to lead and guide us. In the face of opposition, we need the Spirit's living water to give us both comfort and discernment in handling our challenges.

The Israelite people would need this help to navigate the opposition ahead.

Finish Numbers 21 by scanning verses 21-35, and record anything that stands out to you:

Here are a few things I noticed. In the midst of opposition:

- Moses tried a diplomatic approach first.
- The people used their sense and abilities by exploring the land before attacking it.
- God repeated the refrain, "Do not be afraid."

How could any of these truths apply to a difficulty you are facing?

When battles come our way, we can learn from the people of Israel to use diplomacy and good sense before charging into war.

When battles come our way, we can learn from the people of Israel to use diplomacy and good sense before charging into war. God doesn't want us to cower in fear. We can use our God-given abilities and rely on the Lord to fight our fears in battle. This is the path to contentment even when it seems that everyone else is against us.

God's Word is so rich in truth. I hope you have loved exploring these Old Testament foreshadowings of Christ as much as I have. Today we grew a bigger view of Him as our daily bread, the one who was lifted up to save us from sin and death, and the living water. I pray these truths will sink deeper into our minds and hearts as we continue learning about contentment in the midst of opposition.

Talk with God

Spend some time in prayer focusing on God's attributes. Write a list in the margin describing who God is and/or what He has done in your life.

DAY 2: MORE THAN MEETS THE EYE

Today's Scripture Focus

Numbers 22

George Mueller was born in Germany in the early 1800s. By his own words he referred to himself as a liar and a thief who spent much of his early years at university half intoxicated. When a friend invited him to a Bible study, the course of his entire life changed. He traveled to London hoping to join a missionary service and travel overseas, but he ended up pastoring the same church in England for over sixty-six years. However, George Mueller is most known for his work with orphans. He built five large orphan houses that cared for more than ten thousand children over the course of his lifetime.

Throughout his ministry, George endured much opposition. When he first presented the idea of purchasing a home to house and care for orphans, a woman from his own church came up afterward to tell him that it seemed financially impossible. Against all logic, George believed that God would provide. On one occasion George was seated at a table of children and thanked God for dinner while knowing there was no food. Then came a knock at the door, and there stood an unexpected visitor who had felt nudged by God to bring bread and provisions. George prayed and expectantly believed. His actions and prayer life revealed his theology of a God who intervenes in the lives of His children.[1]

Today we'll examine a biblical story that reveals similar themes of divine intervention—one that is both humorous and deadly serious. In this story we'll find an incredible reminder that when it comes to our battles in this world, there is more than meets the eye.

Read Numbers 22:1-6 and answer the following questions:

Why was Balak, king of Moab, terrified by the Israelites? (vv. 2-4)

Because of his fear, who did Balak send for and why? (vv. 5-6)

Balak knew that he was outnumbered and that Israel's God was helping them. Conventional warfare would not save his people, so he turned to a soothsayer with spiritual powers. While we don't know much about Balaam, commentator Warren Wiersbe has said, "He had a reputation for success in divination (receiving hidden knowledge, especially about the future) and incantation (the use of occult power to grant blessing or cursing), and he was willing to sell his services to all who could pay his fee."[2]

Balak sent for a diviner for hire, but God's people were strictly forbidden from fortune-telling, witchcraft, sorcery, or interpreting omens (see Leviticus 19:26, 31 and Deuteronomy 18:10). Though we likely do not struggle with a temptation to call the local soothsayer to curse our enemies, we must recognize the role of the spiritual world around us. Ephesians 6:12 tells us that there are ranks of evil forces in the spiritual realm—principalities, powers, rulers, and spiritual hosts (NKJV). As followers of Christ, we must be discerning as we live in a world that is both physical and spiritual. God is greater than any evil power, but Scripture cautions us to avoid unholy spiritual practices.

What are some practical ways Christ-followers can discern inappropriate spiritual practices?

The gals in my pilot group for this study came up with some great suggestions:

- Ask God in prayer to give you spiritual discernment regarding specific situations or activities.
- Search the Scriptures for truth and wisdom to identify counterfeits or false teaching.
- Pay attention to your gut reaction; it can alarm you that something isn't right.
- Ask someone with the spiritual gift of discernment for wisdom.

We can look to Scripture to identify some things that are expressly forbidden. Other practices might be gray areas where we wrestle in prayer and ask the Holy Spirit to guide us.

Let's read on and see how the story unfolds in the next verses.

Read Numbers 22:7-20, and summarize in a few phrases or sentences Balaam's response to the delegates who came with money on two occasions:

At first it may seem that Balaam was a follower of Israel's God since he dialogued with Yahweh and seemed to follow His directives. However, each nation had its own god, so Balaam would have sought Yahweh simply because He was the God of the Israelites. Balaam asked God questions, but that didn't mean he was a worshiper. We get a glimpse into his motives as we find references to him in the New Testament.

Write a word or phrase to describe Balaam according to each passage:

2 Peter 2:15

Jude 11

Revelation 2:14

For a man known for his spiritual power, Balaam certainly was influenced by the lure of earthly things such as money, idols, and sexual immorality. We can add these things to our growing list of contentment killers. The desire for instant gratification keeps us in a cycle of wanting more, but lasting calm will not develop in our souls as the result of increased money, idolatry, or pleasure.

In what ways do you see the pursuit of money, idolatry, or pleasure contributing to less contentment in our culture?

> **We must guard against greed so that we can find true riches.**

While the battle for more is all around us, we also must fight the battle individually. John D. Rockefeller was an industrialist and the founder of the Standard Oil Company. He is known as one of the richest men who ever lived. It is reported that when he was asked, "How much money is enough money?" he replied, "Just a little bit more."[4] That is a sentiment shared by many today.

If we aren't careful, we can catch the disease of Balaam. We must guard against greed so that we can find true riches.

Read 1 Timothy 6:6-8 in the margin. What is great wealth or gain?

> *True godliness with contentment is itself great wealth. After all, we brought nothing with us when we came into the world, and we can't take anything with us when we leave it. So if we have enough food and clothing, let us be content.*
>
> *(1 Timothy 6:6-8)*

According to these verses, we should be content if we have enough of what two things?

Write a brief prayer below to thank God for the food and clothing He has provided for you and let Him know that you are satisfied with what you have.

Great wealth is just around the corner for those who practice godliness with contentment. The riches may or may not be monetary, but their value exceeds anything Rockefeller could have imagined.

Let's return to Balaam's story. Read Numbers 22:21-41, and summarize what happened in your own words:

Extra Insight

Donkeys have long been known for their stupidity and obstinacy: "Do not be like a senseless horse or mule / that needs a bit and bridle to keep it under control" (Psalm 32:9).

God blocked Balaam's way with an angel and made his donkey speak, which caused Balaam to listen to the angel and agree to say only what God told him. Through this story, the Lord reminds us that there often is much more than meets the eye when it comes to our own battles. There is a supernatural realm, and the Lord of heaven's armies is on our side in the midst of opposition.

How does knowing that God can block the path with an angel and talk through a donkey impact any fears or worries you've been experiencing lately?

All too often our human logic and emotion take over, and our situations can seem insurmountable at times. We think we will never get out from under our debt. We fret over whether our children really will be all right. The "what ifs" and "if onlys" can creep into our thinking continually. But the story of Balaam (which we'll continue tomorrow) reminds us that even when others are out to get us, our God is on our side. He is the Lord of heaven's armies.

> Read the words of Ephesians 6:12 in the margin. Whom is our battle *not* against?

So often we think it is our friend, coworker, neighbor, spouse, or relative who is opposing us. God reminds us that our battles are spiritual. Our enemy can come as a lion who devours (1 Peter 5:8) or a serpent who deceives (2 Corinthians 11:3), but God is the ultimate victor. We fight our battles from a mind-set of victory.

> Check the principle from our study today that resonates most in your life right now:

__ We must exercise discernment regarding subtle spiritual practices of evil.

__ Greed, idolatry, and immorality are spiritual traps that promise much but deliver little.

__ Contentment comes through gratitude for God's provision rather than longing for more.

__ Knowing that the Lord of heaven's armies is on our side encourages us not to give in to worry or fear.

George Mueller embraced these truths and changed the world through his faith in a supernatural God. Though you're likely not rescuing orphans from the streets of England, God can use you to have an incredible impact in your own sphere of influence!

Talk with God

While you may not hear the Lord through the mouth of a donkey today, thank Him that He can speak to you in any way He chooses. Ask Yahweh to give you ears to hear His voice and eyes to see His supernatural work around you.

Even when others are out to get us, our God is on our side.

We are not fighting against flesh-and-blood enemies, but against evil rulers and authorities of the unseen world, against mighty powers in this dark world, and against evil spirits in the heavenly places.

(Ephesians 6:12)

DAY 3: PERSISTENT OPPOSITION

As I've mentioned, my identical twin daughters both have forms of alopecia, and one of them lost all of her hair at age twelve. After a year she began adjusting to life with wigs and complicated situations such as swimming and sleepovers. It felt like our family was finally coming up for air, and then her sister discovered a few bald spots. I wrote in my journal, "Can we just catch our breath, Lord?"

Have you ever had one problem in your life resolve only to find another one coming up to take its place? It can seem that if it's not one thing, it's another. Life is full of challenges, and sometimes opposition appears to be persistent in our lives. It can feel like we are fighting an uphill battle in our pursuit of intimacy with God and the contentment that brings. In just the last week I've fought a tough parenting situation, a stomach virus, worry and fear about the future, neck and back pain, fatigue, temptation to judge someone who hurt me, and criticism from strangers who misunderstood the intent of my words. Taylor Swift tells us to just "shake it off," but that is often easier said than done. Though these situations in my life were just passing skirmishes, sometimes we can be fighting an all-out war. I read a friend's online article in which she shared the story of her son's heroin addiction and how that affected her family. My eyes welled with tears as I thought about the daily battles she fought on behalf of those she dearly loves. All of us have challenges, and sometimes we can feel that we're in the thick of a full-fledged war and someone or something is out to get us.

That was exactly what was happening to the armies of Israel. King Balak wanted Balaam to curse the Israelites, and he wasn't giving up easily. He persisted in opposition.

Read Numbers 23:1-12.

According to verses 1-2, what did Balaam tell King Balak to do to try to get a favorable response?

Summarize Balaam's first message or oracle. (vv. 7-10)

Though Balaam was not a worshiper of Yahweh, he knew about the rituals of Israelite worship. He encouraged King Balak to emulate the practice of sacrifice to try to appease the God of Israel. However, neither of them really knew the God of Israel—or the protocol for acceptable sacrifices. As one source points out, "Israelite prophets were never required to offer sacrifices before they received divine messages."[5]

Throughout history we see people parse out "religious pieces" to try to manipulate gods or circumstances to get their own way. A prayer, practice, or sacrifice out of context misses the bigger picture of what it means to truly follow God. With our modern mind-set grounded in rationalism, it can be difficult for us to understand the mystical beliefs these Mesopotamian ancients had related to curses and blessings. They believed in the spirit world in a way that is foreign to us. Balak knew he was outmanned, so he tried to turn Israel's God against them with bribery. Yet God met Balaam and gave him a message Balak did not want to hear.

As we continue to read, we learn much about our God's character.

Read Numbers 23:13-26, and record below anything you discover about God's nature in Balaam's second message or oracle (vv. 18-24), which is a blessing:

Extra Insight

Balaam's blessing uses parallelism poetry indicative of the time period.

God is not like us. He doesn't lie or play games. If He says He will do something, He does it. He is committed to His people. Though He disciplined and corrected His people, blessing was His ultimate desire for them.

Balak was determined to oppose Israel and find a way to curse them, but God didn't relent. As we'll see, Balak kept looking for ways to coerce a curse for the people of Israel even after Balaam had pronounced a blessing. Yet like a stream running down the side of a mountain, God's blessing could not be stopped.

You can try to dam up a mountain stream, but ultimately the water will find its way due to the law of gravity. In the same way, people and difficulties will oppose God's blessing in our lives, but in the end God's blessing will prevail. Embracing this truth will help us learn contentment in a culture of more.

What kind of opposition has threatened to dam up the flow of God's blessings in your life lately?

Friend, just as God delivered His people from slavery in Egypt, He will deliver you! Remember, God does not lie: "Has he ever promised and not carried it through?" (Numbers 23:19c). And God has promised to never leave or forsake you (Hebrews 13:5). These are the truths we cling to when our own King Balaks seem to stop at nothing to oppose us.

Continue reading the story in Numbers 23:27-30. What was Balak's next idea? Where did he take Balaam this time?

Peor was a mountain identified with the pagan god Baal.[6] Verse 28 tells us that it overlooked a wasteland. Perhaps Balak thought this desolate place would help evoke a curse. In any case, he was desperately grasping at straws to curse his enemies. We also have an enemy who opposes us at every turn, yet our God is much greater.

You belong to God, my dear children. You have already won a victory over those people, because the Spirit who lives in you is greater than the spirit who lives in the world.

(1 John 4:4)

Read 1 John 4:4 in the margin. How does this verse encourage you in your current circumstances?

In the next chapter, Numbers 24, we come to Balaam's third message or oracle where we see an emphasis on the contentment the Israelites would experience in the Promised Land.

Read Numbers 24:1-14. According to verses 5-7, what are some tangible things the wilderness wanderers were destined to enjoy?

The Israelites had endured much hardship. They'd lost an entire generation of parents and grandparents because of disobedience. For nearly forty years they had wandered under God's leading, and Yahweh knew exactly where His people were and where they were headed. He planned to bless them, and no Moabite king out to curse them could thwart His blessing. They were destined for beautiful tents, lovely homes, abundant gardens, and strength like that of cedar trees. Water would abound for them. Like a mountain stream, God's blessings would break through any opposition.

You may be saying, "It's great that God blessed the people of Israel, but they were His special, chosen people."

Read Galatians 3:26-29 in the margin, and answer the following questions:

What makes someone a child of God?

Who are the true children of Abraham?

You are all children of God through faith in Christ Jesus. And all who have been united with Christ in baptism have put on Christ, like putting on new clothes. There is no longer Jew or Gentile, slave or free, male and female. For you are all one in Christ Jesus. And now that you belong to Christ, you are the true children of Abraham. You are his heirs, and God's promise to Abraham belongs to you.

(Galatians 3:26-29)

As followers of Christ, we are children of Abraham—God's chosen ones! Whether we face daily struggles, the blahs, physical pain, relational conflicts, or all-out war, God's blessings will win out for us, His children. As we believe these truths and allow them to sink deep into our souls, contentment can't help but grow. The problem is that life's oppositions persist to discourage us. We need faith to cling to contentment in the midst of constant challenges.

What are some practical actions or habits that have helped you cling to the hope of God's blessings in the midst of opposition in your life?

God later called His people to remember the story of Balaam. Nehemiah (Nehemiah 13:2), Micah (Micah 6:5), and several New Testament passages we looked at yesterday mention Balaam. God wanted His people to remember His commitment to bless them.

Read Deuteronomy 23:4-5 in the margin, and circle why God turned the intended curse into a blessing.

God loves us. When opposition heats up in our lives, we can hold firm to the truths we know about God's love and blessing. Just as Balak kept trying to get Balaam to curse Israel, some people never give up. Sometimes one thing after another goes wrong. Yet the psalmist said, "As pressure and stress bear down on me, / I find joy in your commands" (Psalm 119:143). When trials keep coming and coming, we must look to God's Word for His love and promises. The Lord is more determined to bless us than anyone else is to thwart us! We can remember these truths and overcome.

"These nations did not welcome you with food and water when you came out of Egypt. Instead, they hired Balaam son of Beor from Pethor in distant Aram-naharaim to curse you. But the Lord your God refused to listen to Balaam. He turned the intended curse into a blessing because the Lord your God loves you."

(Deuteronomy 23:4-5)

In the remaining verses of Numbers 24, we find Balaam's final messages against enemy nations and also some messianic glimpses of a future king who will rise out of Jacob. While some point to King David's future monarchy, other commentators suggest these words find ultimate fulfillment in Christ. What we know for sure is that God's will cannot be manipulated or changed by those who oppose us: "Alas, who can survive / unless God has willed it?" (Numbers 24:23). No unfaithful spouse, rebellious child, vengeful friends, unfair employer, or unkind relatives or neighbors can stand in the way of the blessing God has in store for those who follow Him! God is greater than any foe we will ever face!

Talk with God

Include these verses from Psalm 119:142-144 in your prayer time with the Lord:

Your justice is eternal,
and your instructions are perfectly true.
As pressure and stress bear down on me,
I find joy in your commands.
Your laws are always right;
help me to understand them so I may live.

DAY 4: TEMPTATION

We've seen this week that in the face of persistent opposition, God continually blessed His people. Today we will find a caution that rings true in the midst of God's posture of blessing toward us. The danger isn't in God changing and withholding His gracious favor but in us failing to receive it.

This caution goes hand in hand with some lessons about temptation in a difficult passage tucked away in Numbers 25—one I've never seen as a social media meme or a theme for a conference or sermon series. Many of us tend to gravitate toward verses about God's grace and blessing rather than His call to obedience. Our Lord certainly is gracious and loving, but He also shows us clearly His position on sin. He doesn't wink at it, joke about it, or make light of it. Instead, He warns us of the seriousness of it. I pray you'll join me in tackling a sober passage with the intention to know and follow God in a way that lines up with the truth of Scripture—all the while relying mightily on God's Spirit to do the work of obedience in and through us. In the end we will find that when we are traveling the road of destructive sin, the Lord graciously provides off-ramps so that we can exit the path of disobedience. And thanks be to God for His grace!

Yesterday we learned that Balak persistently attempted to procure a curse on the people of Israel, but God gave a supernatural blessing instead. Numbers 24:25 tells us that Balaam left and returned home, but he didn't stay there for long.

Read Numbers 25:1-3, and write a brief description of what happened while the Israelites were camped at Shittim, or Acacia Grove:

The first few verses of Numbers 25 mention that it was the Moabite women who tempted the men of Israel. As we continue in this chapter, however, we will find a Midianite woman being brought into an Israelite man's tent. We saw in Numbers 22:4-7 that the Moabites and Midianites formed an alliance together against Israel. Even though Balaam's involvement in this alliance isn't mentioned here, Numbers 31:18 records that Balaam died among the Midianites. We also discover in Numbers 31 that Moses was furious with his generals and captains for letting the Midianite women live after battle. He says, "These are the very ones who followed Balaam's advice and caused the people of Israel to rebel against the Lord at Mount Peor" (Numbers 31:16a).

So, we learn that it was Balaam who came up with a scheme and counseled the Midianites and Moabites to use their women to tempt the Israelites into sin. Perhaps then he could collect the honorarium from Balak that the Lord prevented him from getting when he was unable to curse the people. A verse in Revelation supports this premise.

Read Revelation 2:14 in the margin. According to this verse, what were the two ways that Balaam taught the people of Israel to sin:

1.

2.

Idolatry and immorality poison the soul by leading individuals and communities away from God instead of toward Him. The lure of idolatry for the people of Israel isn't so different from our own temptations. Let's consider some of the ways we all struggle with counterfeits:

Extra Insight

The Israelites were enticed to go to the mountain of Peor, which is where Balak took Balaam before he gave his third oracle. This is the first recorded instance of the people of Israel worshiping Baal, but sadly it won't be the last. Baal was the most prominent Canaanite deity known for rain and fertility.

"I have a few complaints against you. You tolerate some among you whose teaching is like that of Balaam, who showed Balak how to trip up the people of Israel. He taught them to sin by eating food offered to idols and by committing sexual sin."
(Revelation 2:14)

1. *Sensual stimulation.* Idolatry offers a good feeling in the moment. Decadent foods and sexual pleasure were part of most pagan practices, including Baal worship.
2. *Material gain.* Possessions and wealth offer the false promise of security. Baal worship specifically promised rain for crops and fertility for animals and people. Both of these offered the promise of wealth when crops and livestock multiplied.
3. *Tangible symbols.* Trusting in a God you cannot see or touch can be difficult. In Exodus, the Israelites made a golden calf when Moses took too long on the mountain. When God seems silent, it can be tempting to look to more concrete options than an invisible God.
4. *Social pressure.* When everyone around us seems to be giving in to counterfeits that promise temporary pleasure, we can be tempted to excuse our deviation from God's clear commands. The polytheism that surrounded Israel in many nations, including Moab and Midian, influenced Israel toward inclusive tolerance rather than single-minded devotion to Yahweh.

In the same way, we face temptations of momentary pleasure and greed. We long for comfort, pleasure, and indulgence of the flesh—much as the people of Israel did. We must ask ourselves where the influences around us might be leading us to compromise the truths we know from God's Word. Commentator Roy Gane has said, "Worshiping God improperly results in a distorted view of him."[8] The converse is also true: having a distorted view of God results in improper worship. So, we must see God clearly so that we can know and worship Him.

Take a moment to consider where any counterfeits have crept into your heart and mind. As you look at the four struggles with idolatry listed above, put a star beside any that you can relate to in your own battles with counterfeits.

It's good to take time to reflect and see where we might be headed off course, even if only in our thinking. We all have blind spots. We don't usually make drastic changes away from worshiping God. Often it is a slow fade.

Write a brief prayer below asking the Lord to reveal any areas of idolatry or immorality that might be hindering your intimacy with Him:

Now continue the story by reading Numbers 25:4-18, and write any reactions or questions you have below:

OK, I'm with you! This is difficult to read. I know God is loving and gracious, so this seems extreme. However, I know that all Scripture is inspired by God and useful for teaching us. So rather than sit in my *Why*? it is better to ask *What can I learn*?

We can have such a bent toward God's love and grace that we fail to balance it with His holiness and justice. God had given His people the Ten Commandments, and their behavior went against those clear commands. The first commandment cautioned them to worship no other gods but Him, the second forbade idolatry, and the seventh instructed them not to commit adultery. Not only had many of the people disobeyed God's moral code; Zimri then brazenly took a Midianite woman into his tent before everyone as an act of rebellion against God, and it angered Yahweh. Zimri was a chieftain's son who perhaps thought his high position meant he didn't have to follow the clear commands of God.

Rather than get tripped up with the details, let's remember to look for the warning for us. Sin is serious. Immorality, idolatry, and compromise are dangerous. Phinehas was a priest whose job was to represent God to the people. Because he was aligned with God's heart for holiness and purity, His anger mirrored divine anger. The sins of these Israelites were a serious breach of covenant loyalty.

Read Psalm 106:28-31 in the margin, and underline any words used to describe Phinehas.

God regarded Phinehas's act, which stopped the plague, as courageous and described him as righteous. Yet as one commentator notes, "The body count of 24,000, an average of 2,000 from each of the twelve tribes, is the highest ever suffered by the Israelites during their long and painful passage from Egypt to Canaan."[9] I told you this would be a sobering passage!

Let's turn to the New Testament to see how the Apostle Paul used the lesson of Numbers 25 to warn the church at Corinth about these same sins.

Read 1 Corinthians 10:6-8 and briefly describe how Paul said these stories should impact us:

Extra Insight

Jesus also became angry at sin. When He encountered flagrant, unrepentant sin, especially among religious leaders, He got downright mad (see Mark 11:15-17 and John 2:13-17).

*Our ancestors joined in the worship of Baal at Peor;
  they even ate sacrifices
    offered to the dead!
They angered the LORD
with all these things,
  so a plague broke out
    among them.
But Phinehas had the
courage to intervene,
  and the plague was
    stopped.
So he has been regarded
as a righteous man
  ever since that time.*
    (Psalm 106:28-31)

Paul said these stories are a warning to us so we won't crave what they did. We should be careful not to worship idols or engage in sexual immorality. In the next verses we find great news with practical insight.

According to 1 Corinthians 10:12-13, what does God say He will provide for us when we face temptation?

None of us is immune to yielding to temptation. Whether it is having an affair, viewing inappropriate content on the Internet, or allowing other things to take God's place in our lives, we must be careful and remember these warnings. When we assume we could never fall into idolatry or immorality, we are in danger of the pride that keeps us from being on guard.

God says that He will provide an escape route of obedience when we face temptation, but He doesn't say that He will never give us more than we can handle. That is a cliché that misinterprets the intent of these verses. I almost always feel like I am facing more than I can manage in my own strength. Parenting my children, loving my husband, serving at church, and living a holy life definitely feel like more than I can handle most days, and the reality is that they *are*! Jesus said that apart from Him we can do nothing (John 15:5). We need the Lord to overcome sin and live the life He calls us to live. Only He can provide the power required to be His follower. We must recognize our need and yield to Him, believing by faith that He will do the heavy lifting!

When we find ourselves on the path of sin, God shows us the off-ramp.

God reminds us in this passage from 1 Corinthians 10 that He is always faithful. He does not shame, condemn or curse us. He is always on our side. In fact, He will provide a way out for us. When we find ourselves on the path of sin, God shows us the off-ramp. We can turn from our sin and turn to Him.

This is the message I see resounding throughout God's Word, including here in Numbers 25. John the Baptist came preaching it (Mark 1:4), and it was the tone of Jesus' ministry (Matthew 4:17). God calls us to turn from our sin and turn toward Him. He taught this to His people in the wilderness, and He reminds us to look at what happened to them and learn to stay far away from sin.

We've traveled quite a journey with the Israelites in the wilderness, and now they're getting close to the end of that journey and the beginning of a new one. One commentator points out, "The twenty-four thousand Israelites who died in the plague in 25:9 are presumably the last remnants of the old generation. They have left the stage to make room for a new generation who will again stand on the edge of the promised land."[10] God fulfilled His promise to take only the next generation into the land. The remnant left are on the verge of a fresh start. We can make a fresh start today as well by turning from our sin and turning toward our loving and holy God.

Contentment is tough when people around us are enjoying sin. We can easily get drawn into our culture's fascination with sex and idolatry characterized by greed for more stuff. When we are weary from battle is when we are most susceptible to temptation, but the Lord says He will provide the off-ramp. We just need to follow Him off the road to sin, leaning hard into God's instructions for right living with total dependence on the power and strength of His Spirit. With our full surrender, He will not fail us.

Talk with God

Ask the Lord to show you the way out when it comes to the temptations in your life. Though you may not be lured by idolatry or immorality, we all battle a sin nature. Ask the Lord to help you live a victorious life through the power of Christ in you, staying far away from disobedience so that you can draw near to God.

DAY 5: REGROUPING

Today's Scripture Focus

Numbers 26

We've walked with the Israelites through some challenging experiences, seeing that our gracious God is also a holy God who judges sin. Yet as we'll see, God's extravagant mercy often comes on the heels of judgment. As we begin Numbers 26, we shift from punishment to promise as the Israelites prepare to finally take the land after forty years of wandering. Did I hear a hallelujah? Hold on to that excitement, because first they have a bit of regrouping to do before they can step into God's Promised Land.

Today we come to the second census found in Numbers. We read about the first one in chapter 1 as the people prepared for battle.

As you'll recall, the Israelites had failed to obey God's instructions to take the land when the scouts brought back a bad report (Numbers 13). And as a result of their complaining and fear, God had relegated them to wander in the wilderness; only the second generation would be left to actually enter the land (Numbers 14:32-33). The time has now come for God's promises to be fulfilled.

Change has been one of the only constants in the lives of these wilderness wanderers. They have continually been moving. They have obeyed and disobeyed. People have died, and others have been born. Their leaders have aged. In the midst of it all, their shoes have not worn out and their God has been faithful to provide them with daily food (Deuteronomy 29:5-6).

How can you relate to the Israelites in having to adapt to change? Check all that you have experienced:

___ Job transition(s)

___ Moving to a new town

___ Children being born

___ Children leaving home

___ Children returning home.

___ The death of a loved one

___ A change in a relationship

Like the people of Israel, we often find ourselves regrouping due to change. But regrouping can be a time to look ahead with hope-filled expectancy. After seasons of temptation and failure, God reminded His people that although He punishes sin, He never forgets His promises of blessing.

Read Numbers 26:1-4, and note below God's instructions to Moses and Aaron:

On the plains of Moab across from the city of Jericho, God instructed the leaders to count the people and prepare for battle. The necessity for this recounting of the people was twofold according to commentator Warren Wiersbe:

- to know how many men were available, twenty years and older, who could serve in the army;
- to get an idea of how much land each tribe would need when Israel settled down in Canaan and claimed their inheritance.[11]

So, this census was taken in anticipation of entering the long-awaited Promised Land. Moses prepared the people for the battles ahead even though he knew he would not be joining them. The first generation had complained about their circumstances often and looked back on their former slavery with inaccurate lenses. After regrouping, the new generation would have their own choice—they could complain about their challenges or obey

God in faith. In the same way, when we go through seasons of change, we should regroup and prepare for the good things God has planned for the future.

We've learned throughout our study not to get stuck in the past. As you contemplate your own changing circumstances, where might the Lord be calling you to learn from the past while looking forward rather than backward?

The experiences and pain from the past can be an excellent tutor, but we cannot wallow in their company too long. Regrouping helps us learn from the past while preparing for what is to come.

If we skim through Numbers 26:5-57, we notice a few differences in this census compared to the previous one taken in Numbers 1:

- The second census totaled 601,730 soldiers for battle, while the first had been 603,550. When we consider that an entire generation died in the wilderness, we see that God blessed and multiplied His people with the births of many children in the years of their wandering.
- We see a significant drop in the number of soldiers from Gad, Reuben, and Simeon. The largest decrease was Simeon, going from 59,300 to 22,200. All of these tribes had camped south of the Tabernacle and had experienced the consequences of sin in Korah's rebellion (Numbers 16) and Zimri's brazen adultery accompanied by a plague (Numbers 25).
- Judah, Issachar, and Zebulun showed the largest increases, and all camped together east of the Tabernacle. It seems that both rebellion and blessing were contagious among neighbors.

One redemptive story we find tucked in this census concerns the descendants of Korah.

What do we learn about Korah's sons from Numbers 26:11?

Although Korah rebelled against God by inciting a rebellion against Moses, this is a glimmer of hope for his legacy. Though Korah had enticed 250 prominent leaders to join him and had stirred up the whole community,

> The experiences and pain from the past can be an excellent tutor, but we cannot wallow in their company too long.

apparently his sons did not join him in sin for they did not suffer the fate of all who followed him. Instead, we find the descendants of Korah alive and well in the new generation. As I mentioned last week (Day 3), the descendants of Korah became authors of a number of psalms. One source notes that they authored no less than eleven psalms, and that "these include some of the greatest expression of faith and praise in the Bible, which have inspired some of our most beloved hymns and songs such as Martin Luther's 'A Mighty Fortress' (Psalm 46)."[12]

We serve a God of grace who looks to bring good out of bad situations. Though Korah made poor choices, his children and grandchildren seemed to learn from their ancestor's errors and change their family tree.

As you reflect on your life, when and how have you seen God redeem a bad situation and use it for good?

After forty years of wandering, the second census provides us a sign of God's completed judgment. Take a look for yourself.

Read Numbers 26:63-64, and summarize below how the census shows God's punishment was fulfilled:

Some commentators suggest that the censuses in chapters 1 and 26 serve as structural pillars for the Book of Numbers, with chapters 1–25 as the first segment and Chapter 26 as the beginning of a second part of the wilderness adventure. Commentator Dennis Olson has pointed out that the questions change at this point in the saga. It is no longer "How can a holy and powerful God live among sinful people?" but "How can the second generation be faithful, avoiding the rebellions and disasters of the previous generation?"[13]

We can ask similar questions when we come out on the other side of difficulties and failures. We might ask, "What can we learn from the mistakes of the past so that we can do things differently in the future?" As we consider such questions, we need to keep in mind that regardless of our past sins and mistakes, God's commitment to us remains strong and unchanging; it is our response that is the variable determining whether we accept God's provision and direction.

How has God helped you choose better paths based on past failures, whether made by yourself or others?

The Israelites who were now on the cusp of entering the Promised Land had watched their parents and grandparents disobey, choose fear over faith, worship idols, fall into sexual immorality, and complain. They had witnessed the plagues and punishments that accompanied these behaviors, and now they had an opportunity for a fresh start. We will see many parallels between the tests and instructions given to the first generation in Numbers 1–25 and those given to the new generation in Numbers 26–36. Yet we find an important distinction in Caleb and Joshua. Though most of the first generation's disobedience and rebellion ended in death, we see through Caleb and Joshua that every individual who chooses a life of faith can receive the blessings of obedience. Because of their faith, they were exempt from the punishment given to everyone else in the first generation.

Read Galatians 6:7-9 in the margin. How do these verses support God's interaction with Joshua and Caleb?

As you reflect on these verses in relation to your own life, where is God calling you to "not become weary in doing good"?

Do not be deceived: God cannot be mocked. A man reaps what he sows. Whoever sows to please their flesh, from the flesh will reap destruction; whoever sows to please the Spirit, from the Spirit will reap eternal life. Let us not become weary in doing good, for at the proper time we will reap a harvest if we do not give up.

(Galatians 6:7-9 NIV)

As we transition through the changes in our own lives, we need to take stock of what we have and what we've lost. Change can be difficult, and often we must regroup to find our new normal. But as we do this, we can learn valuable lessons from the past so that we do not repeat mistakes in the future. And that positions us to enter into the land of God's blessing.

Talk with God

Reflect on the opposition you've faced in your life. Ask God to make clear what He wants to teach you through it and what new behaviors and patterns you can take with you into the future.

Digging Deeper

God asked the people to take a census on two occasions in the Book of Numbers, but later God would punish King David for counting his fighting men. Check out the online Digging Deeper article for Week 5, "Context" (see AbingdonWomen.com/NumbersDigging Deeper) to see that not all of God's instructions are binding in every situation. Context is important as we interpret Scripture.

Weekly Wrap-Up

As we end this week, take a moment to review what we've studied. Flip back through the lessons and write something from each day that resonated with you that you can apply in your life.

Day 1: Occupied Territory

_____

Day 2: More Than Meets the Eye

_____

Day 3: Persistent Opposition

_____

Day 4: Temptation

_____

Day 5: Regrouping

_____

Contentment Clue: **Perseverance**

We learn contentment by persevering when the journey is long and we grow weary.

_____ is everything when it comes to fighting the battle of contentment.

In order to persevere we must exercise _____.

Numbers 21:4-5 – The people complained about the manna

- *Psalm 78:25 – the food of angels*

- *Exodus 16:31 – tasted like honey wafers*

We must lift up our heads and _____ at _____ in the midst of opposition.

Numbers 21:6-9 – the bronze snake

John 3:14-17 – Christ compared to the bronze snake

Greed is an enemy that can _____ and _____ us.

Numbers 22:4-6 – The example of Balak and Balaam

_____ + _____ = great gain!

1 Timothy 6:6-12 – godliness with contentment is great wealth

We can't fight our battles in our own _____.

1 John 5:4 – victory through faith

Deuteronomy 33:26-29 – God rides across the heavens to help you

Week 6

CONTENT IN BLESSINGS

Numbers 27-36

Memory Verse

All praise to God, the Father of our Lord Jesus Christ, who has blessed us with every spiritual blessing in the heavenly realms because we are united with Christ.
(Ephesians 1:3)

DAY 1: MAKING AN APPEAL

Weekly Reading Plan

Deuteronomy 25–34

Today's Scripture Focus

Numbers 27

We've come to the last leg of our journey with the wilderness wanderers. I hope you have been learning contentment in deliverance, preparation, uncertainty, obedience, and perseverance. This week we will focus on contentment when it comes to our blessings. Sometimes we must search for these blessings in order to appreciate them, but that enables us to see the incredible impact that gratitude has on our level of contentment.

One of our blessings is that we have the freedom to come to God with our questions and concerns. After college I lived in Canada for three years, and the snow was unlike anything I had ever witnessed. So although I loved the people, I would be lying if I said I wasn't anxious to get back to the States. My pastor husband felt that God was confirming the call to move when four churches simultaneously inquired about hiring him—and he wasn't even looking for a job. The next challenge came in navigating where to go. We quickly ruled out two options, but the other two seemed like great possibilities. After visiting both places, we still weren't sure. One of the options was in the States, in Ohio, and the other was in another city in Canada. One minute we would feel tugged toward Ohio and the next to the city in Canada. Then it seemed that the work permit for the States wasn't going to work out.

We were at a crossroads, wondering if the immigration issue was a hurdle that we needed to overcome or if the Lord was closing a door. I'm glad we wrestled, prayed, and appealed rather than staying content with the obstacle to returning to the states.

In today's passage we will witness two appeals made by God's people. One was granted, and the other was not. While we must learn to accept God's "no," there also is a time to express our discontent to God and ask for change.

If you could ask God for anything right now knowing that He would grant it, what would it be?

Right now I am asking God for my daughter's hair to grow back, better time management skills, and clear direction for college choices for my kids. God invites us to ask. Jesus said, "You can ask for anything in my name, and I will do it, so that the Son can bring glory to the Father" (John 14:13). God invites us to ask in Jesus' name—which means with His authority and reflecting what we know of His values and purposes—and He promises to answer. Yet according to God's will, that answer could be yes, no, or wait.

Let's explore the "yes" and the "no" that God gave in answer to the appeals of His people and consider what we can learn when we receive these types of answers as well.

Appeal #1: Yes

Read Numbers 27:1-11 and answer the following questions:

Who brought a petition? (v. 1)

To whom did they bring it? (v. 2)

What was their request? (vv. 3-4)

How did Moses determine what to do in this case? (v. 5)

What was the Lord's response? (vv. 7-8)

We know that Moses had taken his father-in-law's advice to refrain from hearing every case personally (Exodus 18:24-26). Instead, he appointed leaders who would hear the small cases, so that only the major ones were brought to him. This case had made its way up through the wilderness court system as a significant issue to be heard.

While women were not treated as equals in most of Mesopotamian cultures, the Lord responded to the plea of these daughters. It's noteworthy that "as with the other nations of that day, Israel was a strongly masculine society, and fathers left their property to their sons."[1] According to Deuteronomy 21:15-17, the oldest son received a double portion of the inheritance. Men who didn't have sons left their property to the nearest male relative. Daughters received part of the estate when they married and took a dowry along with them. Dowries included clothing, jewelry, money, and furniture—with wealthier families possibly giving land or even cities as part of the wedding gift.[2]

These daughters of Zelophehad made their case based on their father's name. He had been part of the first generation that had died as a result of the disobedience in not taking the land (Numbers 13). However, the girls pointed out that he was not among Korah's rebels. This story provides us with an example of an instance when it is OK not to be content. The daughters knew the law. However, they found it unfair. The fact that this was an important issue for them when no land had even been conquered yet revealed their faith in God's promise of victory to come. They wanted to ensure that their family's name and inheritance didn't cease because of their gender. These women boldly made an appeal for change, and the Lord's decision set a precedent for future generations.

As we study what it means to be content, it's important to acknowledge that the pursuit of contentment does not exclude making appeals for change. In other words, there are some things we should never be content with such as injustice, apathy, or sin. We should never be content with seeing others suffer unfairly, for example, or with choosing selfish pursuits to the neglect of others' needs.

Can you think of anything unfair or unjust in your world right now that you would like to appeal to the Lord to change? If so, write it below:

> **There are some things we should never be content with such as injustice, apathy, or sin.**

My prayer journal is full of things I want to appeal. Cancer has affected so many people I love. I appeal to the Lord to ease their suffering. I also ask the Lord to act on behalf of the children my family sponsors in Guatemala and the Dominican Republic. And there are so many examples where justice is needed in our world. One of the gals in the pilot group defined justice as "all people having access to the resources necessary to flourish." We can ask God for justice on behalf of so many in our world who don't have clean water, healthy food, or adequate education to flourish. We should appeal when rules are unfair or situations are toxic.

In my own life, I don't want to be content with unhealthy eating habits, poor time management, or unkind words. In our relationships at home, work, or in the community, we sometimes must appeal to others to treat us respectfully or make exceptions to rules. That is when it is important to know the difference between unhealthy worry and healthy concern. Concern is actionable; worry is not. The daughters of Zelophehad had a concern about their father's name and their future in the Promised Land, and they brought their request through proper channels. If they had merely worried about it, perhaps while complaining to others, then their circumstances would not have changed.

Have you ever heard someone complain about injustice or rudeness but refuse to take the time or the risk to address the problem? Worrying and complaining without demonstrating concern through appropriate action is a waste of time. So, let's act on our concerns and not waste our breath starting negative conversations.

Appeal #2: No

As we move into the next part of Chapter 27 and the second appeal, we find the flip side of the Lord's response—a "no." Sometimes we must learn to graciously accept a request denied. That is not to say that learning to be content means accepting unfair treatment or the status quo. Rather, it requires asking, seeking, knocking, and then accepting the decisions God makes.

According to Numbers 27:12-14, what did the Lord instruct Moses to do?

Now read Deuteronomy 3:23-26, and write below Moses' appeal and God's response:

The appeal of Moses:

The response of the Lord:

Moses made a plea to walk through the land, but the Lord told him not to speak of it anymore. Instead, Moses was to be content with a glimpse of the land of promise from Pigsah Peak. I would imagine this might have been difficult to swallow. Moses had led these stubborn people, settled their disputes, listened to their complaints, and pled for mercy on their behalf. He did all of this to lead them out of Egypt and into the land of promise.

Now read Numbers 27:15-17, and write below what Moses was most concerned about after learning of his approaching death:

What we don't find here is a pouting Moses! He didn't play the martyr, saying "woe is me" or "God isn't fair." Instead, he accepted his consequences and shifted his concern to the people. Moses spoke words of blessing to the Lord as the God who gives breath to all creatures. He prayed for his replacement, genuinely desiring a godly man to lead the people. He even expressed his desire that the people not be like a sheep without a shepherd.

A friend of mine told me a story from her trip to Israel. As their leader was teaching them on a hillside, he spoke about shepherds and how they lead out front with the sheep following behind. However, as they traveled down a road later, she noticed a man prodding a group of sheep from behind. When she inquired about this, the leader said that that man wasn't a shepherd but a butcher.

The voice of the shepherd leads by example with gentleness; the voice of the butcher prods sheep toward destruction. Sheep must be led with a gentle but firm hand. Moses wanted these families to come into the Promised Land with someone who would lead them well.

According to Numbers 27:18-23, who did the Lord appoint as the new leader in Moses' place?

What do you remember about Joshua from the story of the spies (Numbers 13)?

Joshua was one of only two spies who had believed the Lord in faith. The change of leadership was to be made clear to the people by the laying on of hands (vv. 18). Then the Lord appointed the gradual release of power from Moses to Joshua for a smooth transition (vv. 20-21). I'm sure Moses had to process his emotions and thoughts, but ultimately he set his sights on the higher goal of the community.

Extra Insight

Moses was 120 years old when he died (Deuteronomy 31:2; 34:7). He did finally make it to the Promised Land, however, when he appeared to Jesus and His disciples on the Mount of Transfiguration (Matthew 17:1-8).

Describe a time when you asked God for something and the answer seemed to be no:

What principles do you learn from the daughters of Zelophehad and Moses regarding making appeals to God and responding to His answers?

The Lord invites us to come to Him with our requests. My husband, Sean, and I eventually got all the paperwork sorted out and were able to come to the States to minister in Ohio, where we felt the Lord leading us. After months of struggling, we finally felt peace and direction. Philippians 4:6 says, "Don't worry about anything; instead, pray about everything. Tell God what you need, and thank him for all he has done."

In light of all we've studied today, write below at least one request you would like to bring before the Lord right now:

In the coming week, when it comes to this matter where you need clarity, I encourage you to take Philippians 4:6 to heart:

- Don't worry. Ask God if there is an action step you need to take regarding your concern.
- Pray about everything. Keep up your dialogue with the Lord concerning this issue.
- Tell God what you need. He already knows, but He wants to hear from you.
- Thank Him for all He has done. Even if you aren't sure which way to go in this matter, thank God for what you do know.

And remember, we know that God is *always* good!

Talk with God

Take some time now to pray and ask the Lord for clear guidance regarding any crossroads you might be facing. Whether it has to do with a job, a relationship, or how to spend your time and money, God wants to hear from you!

DAY 2: MANAGING OUR BLESSINGS

Today's Scripture Focus

Numbers 28 and 29

Blessings come in all shapes and sizes. Children are a blessing from the Lord (Psalm 127:3), as are other relationships. Food, comfort, friendship, and sleep can all be blessings. Sometimes our trials become blessings as we draw close to Jesus through our pain. Other blessings are material. God blesses us with talents and gifts that enable us to work and earn money. Other times He increases our wealth by blessing our efforts or giving us opportunities.

God promised to bless His people in the land of promise. He would give them land and homes and multiply their flocks. We live in a land where most of us have much more than we need. Remember that the Apostle Paul said that if we have enough food and clothing, we should be content (1 Timothy 6:8). He also told the Philippian church, "This same God who takes care of me will supply all your needs from his glorious riches, which have been given to us in Christ Jesus" (Philippians 4:19).

What are some of the blessings the Lord has given you materially beyond food and clothing?

At times we can become so busy managing our blessings that we forget to offer them up to God. We can even complain about the task of maintaining and managing the good things God has given us. Have you ever heard statements like these?

- "I'm so stressed out with my children's schedules and activities."
- "It's so hard to connect at church with us being on the go so much."
- "What a rough day. I had to get an oil change, pay my bills, clean the house, and fertilize the lawn."
- "My supervisor has given me more responsibility at work."

Imagine how those complaints would sound to a family living in a hut in a Third World country. Working with teenagers, I often refer to the novel *The Hunger Games*. Many students have read this book for school or watched the movie based on the book. In it the people of the Capitol are so extravagant, coloring their skin and eating delicacies and being obsessed with fashion, while the people living in other districts are barely surviving. When I mention

> **Each of our blessings is meant to be a gift we treasure and offer up to the Lord rather than one more thing we have to manage.**

to students that we can be compared to the people in the Capitol, while the rest of the world is struggling for daily food, many of them realize how very spoiled and entitled we can be.

Each of our blessings is meant to be a gift we treasure and offer up to the Lord rather than one more thing we have to manage. Today we'll find that the Lord knows blessings carry a latent danger. We must be intentional to remember that the Lord is the source of all our blessings, because we have a tendency to hoard our blessings or find our identity in them.

These next chapters in Numbers interrupt the flow of the narrative. The instructions might seem out of place as the Lord reiterates commands He has given previously (Exodus 29:38-41; Leviticus 1–7). However, the Lord never repeats Himself without good reason. Here we see that He reminded the wilderness wanderers they were not ordinary people entering an ordinary land. They were blessed.

Skim Numbers 28:1-15, and write some of the times the people would need to bring offerings:

These offerings were perpetual reminders for the people to respond to their God with gratitude. There was no other God who created everything, worked miracles, tabernacled with them, provided supernatural food, and made good on His promises. By offering daily, weekly, and monthly sacrifices, they would institute a rhythm of life to help them with thankfulness.

While home maintenance might not be our favorite activity, we can be grateful we have a place to live. Though more responsibility at work might be challenging, we can be thankful we have a job. Driving children around to practices might become boring with all of the waiting, but we can thank God for the lessons and opportunities we can offer them.

God instituted this plan for worship that involved a lot of blood and sacrifice. In history, the wilderness wanderers stood on the other side of the cross of Christ. These offerings pointed toward ultimate sacrifice and redemption through the blood of Christ. They were a temporary covering to remind the people of God's holiness and their own sinfulness.

Sacrifices such as these after the cross would be redundant and unnecessary because they were shadows that pointed to Christ. But to the Israelites who lived before the cross, they reminded the people of the blessing of God's grace. The emphasis on offerings in Numbers reminds us of the enormity of Christ's ultimate sacrifice on our behalf.

Under the new covenant, the need for these sacrifices is obsolete. However, God still calls us to spiritual rhythms to help us keep our blessings in perspective.

Read Romans 12:1-2 in the margin. What is our sacrifice as believers?

The Lord asks us to give ourselves wholeheartedly to Him. We worship Him by offering our lives to Him, seeking His way over our own desires and feelings. We ask God to transform us by aligning our thoughts with His. We put our energy into knowing God's will for us, believing by faith that it is good.

What are some practical ways we can offer our bodies and our lives as living sacrifices?

One of the ways we can do this is to set aside time daily, weekly, and monthly to worship. We might meet with God daily to pray and listen, attend weekly worship services, or celebrate Communion monthly. Under the new covenant, sacrificial practices or spiritual rhythms are not as rigid or fixed as in the old covenant regimen. Because of this some might say that grace is "messier" than law, but it brings freedom.

We notice that the Lord would give them land but also require them to rest weekly in order to enjoy the blessing of that land. This concept hits close to home for me. Our culture moves at such a fast pace. Rest is not part of the regular flow. Yet we are called not to be conformed to this world but to listen to God's way.

How are you doing? Do you find yourself *managing* your blessings or taking the time to *relish* them? God Himself is our greatest blessing, yet so often we lose the wonder of His grace. God knows we struggle with forgetfulness and tend to default to blessing management instead of wonder. So it's not surprising that He instituted special holy days of remembrance for His people.

In Numbers 28:16-31, we find offerings for Passover and the Festival of Harvest (sometimes referred to as Weeks). Then in Numbers 29, we learn about the Feast of Trumpets, the Day of Atonement, and the Feast of Tabernacles.

Dear brothers and sisters, I plead with you to give your bodies to God because of all he has done for you. Let them be a living and holy sacrifice—the kind he will find acceptable. This is truly the way to worship him. Don't copy the behavior and customs of this world, but let God transform you into a new person by changing the way you think. Then you will learn to know God's will for you, which is good and pleasing and perfect.

(Romans 12:1-2)

Take a moment to skim through Numbers 28:16-31 and Numbers 29. What were some of the practices incorporated in these festivities?

Did you notice a lot of sacrificial offerings? These were to be offered in addition to the regular daily, weekly, and monthly sacrifices. Some of the festivals followed the agricultural calendar. God combined spiritual worship with everyday life so that their theology could intersect with their reality.

Here is a chart outlining how many animals were required for the burnt offerings and purification or sin offerings:

Occasion	# of days	Reference in Numbers	Burnt Offering	Purification/ Sin Offering
Daily	1	28:1-8	2 lambs	
Sabbath	1	28:9-10	2 lambs	
New moon	1	28:11-15	2 bulls, 1 ram, 7 lambs	1 goat
Passover (first day of Unleavened Bread)	1	28:16	(see below)	(see below)
Unleavened Bread	7	28:17-25	14 bulls (2 each day), 7 rams total (1 each day), 49 lambs (7 each day)	7 goats (1 each day)
Festival of Harvest (Weeks)	1	28:26-31	2 bulls, 1 ram, 7 lambs	1 goat
Festival of Trumpets	1	29:1-6	1 bull, 1 ram, 7 lambs	1 goat
Day of Atonement	1	29:7-11	1 bull, 1 ram, 7 lambs	1 goat
Festival of Shelters (Booths, Tabernacles)	8	29:12-40	71 bulls (numbers vary by days), 15 rams (2 each day except 1 on the last day), 105 lambs (14 each day except 7 on the last day)	8 goats (1 each day)

God said all of these sacrifices would be a "pleasing aroma" to Him. Offering these sacrifices would give His people time to reflect and appreciate their abundance. God's design for "holy days" always incorporated rest, relationship, and ritual. The purpose of it all was to remember Him. All three elements were needed to help His people reflect and rediscover their wonder for God and their gratitude for His blessings. Yet even while celebrating a holy day to the Lord, the people could lose the wonder of God that it was intended to instill. The same thing can happen in our spiritual holiday celebrations.

How do your spiritual holiday celebrations give you time to reflect on God and His blessings?

What is the next spiritual holiday coming up on your calendar?

In your times of celebration, how can you practically focus on God's intention for us to respond to His wonder with rest, relationship, and ritual?

Extra Insight

It was on the last day of the Feast of Booths (Tabernacles) that Jesus stood in the temple and invited the spiritually thirsty to come to Him (John 7:37-38).

God was going to bless their socks off in this new land. So, in advance He wanted them to see that it all comes from Him. He asked them to offer back to Him just a portion of the blessings they would receive so that they could remember the source of it all.

Just as the Israelites had a regular pattern of sacrifice, we too must continually offer ourselves to God as our spiritual service of worship. With a heart overflowing with contentment in God's provision, we can offer God the best of what we have and pour blessings out on others. This leads to a satisfaction we could never find by managing our blessings and spending them only on ourselves!

Talk with God

Ask the Lord to help you see where you might be managing instead of pouring out His blessings. Offer yourself today as a living sacrifice, willing to go anywhere He leads.

> With a heart overflowing with contentment in God's provision, we can offer God the best of what we have and pour blessings out on others.

DAY 3: FIGHTING FOR EACH OTHER

We learned in Week 1 that Numbers is a book of warfare. In order to be content in our blessings, which is the focus of this final week in our study, we must wage a war against complacency, temptation, and isolation. And because God created us to live in community, He wants us to come alongside each other to help support and defend each other. Fighting for each other does not always come easily. In fact, fighting against each other is often what seems to come naturally. As we've seen, that certainly was the case with the first generation of wilderness wanderers. Here's a review of just a few instances of their grumbling and arguing:

- The people complained about the food. (Numbers 11)
- Miriam and Aaron criticized Moses for his choice of wife and use of power. (Numbers 12)
- The ten spies stirred up the people to have fear rather than faith in taking the land. (Numbers 13)
- The people protested against their leaders. (Numbers 14)
- Korah led others to rise up against Moses because they desired more authority. (Numbers 16)

Like the wilderness wanderers, we need no training in fighting against each other. Criticism, complaining, and gossip come naturally to our flesh and bring division. What we need to learn is how to fight *for* each other. We'll find in Numbers 30–32 three ways that the Lord calls us to fight. Let's consider each one together.

Extra Insight

There is a difference between biblical vows and oaths. "The vow was a promise to do a certain thing for the Lord, while the oath was a promise not to do a certain thing."[3]

Fight for the Truth

First, God calls us to fight for the truth in our relationships. Our God doesn't break promises. What He commits, He completes. We see this clearly in this point of the Israelite's story. In bringing them into the land, Yahweh was fulfilling a promise He had made to Abraham.

God knows, however, that we aren't always good at making good on our own commitments. We sometimes make rash vows. So in Numbers 30, we find that God gave the Israelites some specific instructions regarding vows or pledges where people had promised to abstain from something (similar to the Nazirite vow in Numbers 6) or to offer something to God, such as a gift or sacrifice.

Skim through Numbers 30, and write below anything that stands out to you:

As modern readers, we might think this passage seems demeaning to women. We have to understand that in a patriarchal society, males acted as the primary providers for women. Life for a widow or divorcee was much more difficult in that time. Women today can enjoy financial and legal freedoms that these women wouldn't have been able to comprehend.

In the Bible, we often find the Lord applying divine principles to whatever cultural norms surrounded the hearers. While much of the dialogue in Numbers 30 seems to center around women's vows and the ability of a father or husband to object to anything rash, the main theme is found at the beginning of the chapter.

What is God's instruction regarding vows according to Numbers 30:2?

God reminded the Israelites to be people of their word. Knowing that God heard their vows provided a motivation to refrain from deception. Whether pertaining to men or women, the chapter is dedicated to integrity.

Read Ecclesiastes 5:2 in the margin and write in your own words the instructions regarding vows:

Don't make rash promises, and don't be hasty in bringing matters before God. After all, God is in heaven, and you are here on earth. So let your words be few.

(Ecclesiastes 5:2)

How is the Holy Spirit nudging you to apply these principles of integrity in your life? Is there an area where you need to be true to your word or a situation where you need to use fewer words?

As we consider fighting for the truth in our relationships by honoring our words, we need to put Numbers 30 in a new covenant context. While sacrifices and special vows were very much a part of the old covenant, we find Jesus weighing in on this topic in the Sermon on the Mount.

Read Matthew 5:33-37 in the margin, and write below a sentence summarizing Jesus' instructions:

We can learn to be careful about our commitments. In order to live in community, we need to take time to consider our "yes."

Where or how is the Lord calling you to think about your "yes" and "no" when it comes to any decisions facing you?

Are there words you have spoken that you need to follow through with action? If so, write any action steps below:

Fight for Purity

Our next battle as we prepare for blessings in community has to do with purity. We tend to think of purity as a personal battle, and it is. But purity also is a battle in which we can support and defend each other. The Lord knows that times of abundance can carry with them temptations to compromise.

In Numbers 31, we see that the Lord instructed Moses to attack the Midianites as retribution for their role in leading the Israelites into idolatry and immorality.

Read Numbers 31:1-8, and write a familiar name found in verse 8:

In Numbers 23:10, Balaam had spoken the words, "Let me die like the righteous" in reference to the descendants of Jacob. He wanted to die the death of the righteous, but he didn't live the life of the righteous.

According to Numbers 31:16, what part had Balaam played in tempting Israel?

Chapter 31 records a harsh account of God's judgment on the Midianites. The genocide here can be tough to swallow. One commentator has said, "It is pointless either to defend or condemn God (cf. Job 40:2). Our attempts at theodicy—justifying God's character—are stimulating exercises, but in the final analysis we can only stand back and let God be God, admitting that our reasonings are flawed by inadequate perspective."[4] We don't always understand God's mysterious ways, but we have enough information about His character to know that we can trust Him.

This battle was a dress rehearsal for the war the people of Israel would soon fight to take the Promised Land. The Lord instructed the Israelites to wipe out the Midianites, and Israel divided the plunder and made offerings to the Lord. One change we see in this account is that the people were not complaining but were beginning to walk by faith. God said to take only 12,000 men, and they did not put on their giant or grasshopper glasses in protest as they had done in the past. Instead, they followed the Lord's instructions.

According to Numbers 31:21-24, in what ways were they to purify what they brought into their camp?

Cleansing and purification were important concepts for God's people even as they received plunder. The Lord wanted them to consider what they were bringing into their midst. He wanted them to remember that there is a difference between clean and unclean. The soldiers may have brought in articles used in Midianite idol worship, but God wanted to redeem and purify what had been used for evil. In the same way, we must consider what we are bringing into our midst. As a nation blessed with so much material goods and technology, we can take the time to consider how the Lord would want us to redeem things that are often used for evil in our world.

Reflect for a moment on what enters your heart and mind through each of the following, and write your thoughts:

The Internet

Television

The mailbox

Your phone

The sheer volume of all the images and information streaming into our lives can be overwhelming. In order to embrace contentment in our

"The Israelites capture a fantastic amount of booty [from Midian], a sign of God's faithfulness to this new generation and a foretaste of the conquest of Canaan that is yet to come."[5]

Extra Insight

1. Not one of the 12,000 Israelites died in the battle against Midian (Numbers 31:49). By fighting the battle God's way, miraculous things began to happen!

---

2. The phrase, "be sure your sin will find you out" comes from Numbers 32:23 (KJV) when Moses warned the tribes of Reuben, Gad, and the half tribe of Manasseh to keep their promises and fight for their fellow Israelites.

blessings of technology, we must take the time to consider the impact on our souls. What if we offered up to the Lord all the blessings coming our way and asked Him to purify and cleanse our gifts? What if we were on guard for how our blessings might pollute our nearness to the Lord? How would this, in turn, affect those around us? One way to fight for each other is to battle for purity in our own lives.

Our righteousness comes now through Christ rather than fire or water. Christ calls us to take part in making right choices. Like Balaam, we may desire to die like the righteous, but we must be willing to live for God.

Look up 1 Thessalonians 4:7, and write this short verse below:

Write below any nudges from the Holy Spirit you are hearing regarding any impurity in your life:

Remember, God isn't looking to shame us but to convict us and redirect our course. He hates sin because it destroys us. The Father sent His Son to save the world, not condemn it (John 3:17). Romans 8:1 reiterates that there is no condemnation for those who are in Christ Jesus. Discussions of purity should not cause self-deprecation but a renewed desire to turn away from sin and toward God. Purity is a battle worth fighting—for ourselves, our families, and our communities of faith—so that we can enjoy a rich relationship with the Lord.

Fight for Each Other in Our Battles

Finally, as we prepare for blessings in community, we must be willing to help fight each other's battles. After Israel's big win over Midian, the tribes of Reuben and Gad wanted to settle in some land belonging to the Amorites that they saw because it looked like a good place for livestock.

If you have time, read Numbers 32, or you may read these summary points of the chapter:

- The tribes of Reuben and Gad owned vast amounts of livestock. (v. 1)
- They thought the lands of Jazer and Gilead were well suited for livestock, so they asked Moses, Eleazar, and the other leaders to settle there. (vv. 2-5)

- At first Moses was angry, thinking that they wouldn't help fight for the Promised Land and that this behavior would discourage others from crossing the Jordan as well. (vv. 6-15)
- The tribes of Reuben and Gad clarified that they simply wanted to set up shelters for their livestock and security for their wives and children, but they fully intended to go across the Jordan and fight alongside the other tribes until all the land was conquered. (vv. 16-19)
- Moses then agreed to their plan but warned them of consequences from the Lord if they didn't follow through in battling alongside the other tribes. (vv. 20-24)
- The tribes of Gad and Reuben committed to do as the Lord commanded and serve the people by fighting for the Lord to enter the land of promise. (vv. 25-32)
- Half of the tribe of Manasseh also joined Reuben and Gad in this initiative. They all fought against the Amorites and other Canaanites and renamed the towns. (vv. 33-42)

While some have argued that these tribes compromised by settling for less on the other side of the Promised Land, the main application I see for us is the need to be committed to fight for each other in the body of Christ. We do need to prioritize the care of our families, but we should stay committed to fighting for each other in the battles that come against us. When others are fighting for their marriages, against addiction, or whatever their challenges may be, we can't stand off in the distance and say, "It's not my problem."

Moses warned these tribes about stopping short of working together so that every one of the wilderness wanderers could receive the blessings the Lord had for them. Moses gave a long warning for those unwilling to help others fight their battles.

As you listen to the Holy Spirit, who comes to mind who may need your help and support as they face their challenges?

Can you think of a practical way you can encourage them?

> **When others are fighting for their marriages, against addiction, or whatever their challenges may be, we can't stand off in the distance and say, "It's not my problem."**

Extra Insight

We find in the Book of Joshua (4:12; 22:1-6) that the tribes of Reuben, Gad, and the half-tribe of Manasseh kept their word and fought the Canaanites until the main opposition was defeated. Joshua blessed them to return to their land and reminded them to obey all the Lord's commands.

Through Numbers 30–32, we find that fighting for each other requires us to fight for truth, for purity, and each other's battles. I know the Lord has challenged me to keep my eyes and heart open to see those around me who might need a friend and advocate as they fight their battles. I pray He is doing the same for you.

Talk with God

Ask the Lord to give you His strength and energy as you seek to fight for your sisters and brothers in Christ by living a life of integrity, purity, and sacrifice. Spend some time listening to Him for direction in all three of these areas so that you can fully obey Him and enjoy His blessings in community!

Today's Scripture Focus

Numbers 33–35

DAY 4: REMEMBERING

I love to make photo books and look at pictures from past vacations because it gives me an opportunity to savor the blessings we experienced as a family. The long car rides and sibling squabbles all fade into the background as I remember the sweet memories of meals, shared adventures, and relaxation. As we come to the end of the Book of Numbers, we'll see that the Lord reminded the Israelites of all the amazing things that had transpired to bring them to the edge of the Promised Land. One of the greatest ways to experience contentment involves taking time to stop and count our blessings.

Life is difficult, and the wilderness wanderers had experienced plenty of difficulties: thirst, arguing, death of loved ones, frequent moves, temptation, and opposition from neighboring nations.

What are some of the challenges you have encountered lately? List them below:

In the midst of all the Israelites' problems, God gave them many glimpses of grace—many blessings along the way. He freed them from slavery, led them along the way, reminded them of His presence through the Tabernacle, fed them, gave them water, instructed them in communal living, and used the sacrificial system to foreshadow the ultimate covering for their sin that He would provide through His own Son.

What are some blessings God has provided in your life? List a few that come to mind:

How does recounting these blessings help to bring calm or peace to your soul?

The Israelites had a choice in how they would remember their experiences. They could learn from their mistakes and draw near to God, or they could complain about all the inconveniences and difficulties. We have a similar choice every hour of every day. Though we want to be authentic about our pain, we can choose to strain our eyes to see the goodness of God in the midst of a fallen world.

This is a huge key to contentment. When we count our blessings, we find a lasting calm settling in our souls. But when we dwell in our difficulties and rehearse the injustices in our lives, complaining spills out of the overflow of our hearts and minds. Let's remember along with the Israelites where they have come from as they stand on the edge of the land of promise.

When we count our blessings, we find a lasting calm settling in our souls.

Extra Insight

1. All maps of Israel's wilderness journey, including this one, are best guesses. Places change names over time for social, political, and religious reasons; so the actual locations listed in Numbers 33 are not known. "We do not know for sure where the Israelites crossed the Red Sea, received the law, or ate the manna."[6]

——————

2. Many scholars attribute the authorship of the first five books of the Bible (the Pentateuch) to Moses, and here we find the first mention that Moses wrote things down: "At the LORD's direction, Moses kept a written record of their progress" (Numbers 33:2a).

Skim Numbers 33, and then review this map that outlines the probable travels of the people of Israel:

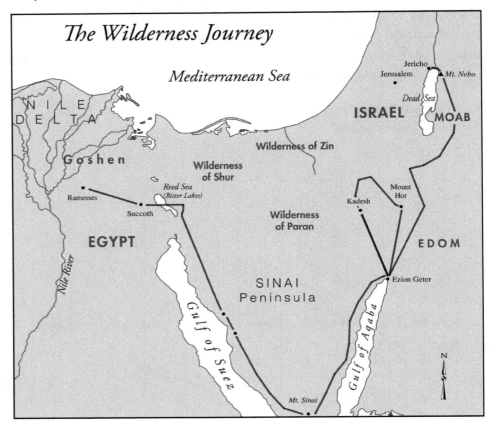

The Wilderness Journey

Notice that the route on the map does not seem to be the most direct. How can you relate to this indirect travel pattern as you consider your own life's journey?

What lessons have you learned about God, yourself, and/or others in seasons that seemed like times of wandering?

After Moses laid out the journey of the past, he then gave some instructions for the people to remember in the future. The blessings of land, leaders, and law would be needed soon. Moses knew he was going to die, and his desire was for the people to flourish during their season of blessing. He wanted them to learn from their mistakes and enjoy their blessings.

Skim Numbers 34 and 35 and write below some of the topics Moses covered:

Why do you think these topics would be important information for God's people in the coming months and years?

While we don't know for sure, I wonder if Moses laid out clear boundaries because he wanted to prevent squabbling over the land. He also gave clarity regarding the identity of each tribal leader to prevent any schism or power struggles after his death. Moses designated towns for the Levites so that each region would have spiritual leadership. He also equipped them with instructions for how to handle assault and murder. Cities of refuge would prevent family feuding and personal vengeance. With no police officers or official justice systems, cities of refuge tempered justice with mercy. These instructions may not seem relevant to us today, but the principles behind them became a huge asset to the people once they settled in the land.

Though we may not be able to apply land boundaries and cities of refuge to our personal lives, we do not lack for biblical instructions to follow. God's Word gives many clear instructions as well as principles for living throughout its pages. I find that when I neglect God's commands regarding things such as rest, forgiveness, prayer, or right living, chaos replaces contentment. For example, when I spend time in prayer, I have more peace. I may not get

Extra Insight

1. "The summary in Numbers 33 is more complete than the accounts in Exodus and earlier in Numbers, which concentrate on places where memorable events have occurred."[7]

2. Israel's territory was the largest during the United Kingdom under the rule of David and Solomon, but even then it did not cover all the territory included in the boundaries set forth by Moses in Numbers 34. "Thus, the portrait of the land is an idealized one that always outdistanced its historical realization."[8]

> **God's boundaries and instructions are intended to guide us and help us navigate our trials and blessings.**

Extra Insight

The process for those accused of murder and the system of the cities of refuge in Numbers 35 show that motives matter to the Lord and impact the punishment given.

everything done, but I enjoy the work, play, and rest the Lord has afforded me with the time that I do have. When I grow complacent in making time with the Lord a priority, I am more prone to engage in worry, shame, and people pleasing.

God's boundaries and instructions are intended to guide us and help us navigate our trials and blessings.

How have the boundaries, rules, and instructions found in God's Word and the promptings of His Holy Spirit brought contentment into your life when you have followed them? Try to think of a specific principle or leading that has protected or helped you personally.

Describe a time when you have not stayed within the Lord's boundaries and followed His instructions that resulted in discontentment:

Obeying God coupled with counting our blessings is a great recipe for contentment. Even when our circumstances are stormy, obedience and thankfulness can bring us a lasting calm. Yet taking the time to review our blessings and God's instructions requires intentionality. The book after Numbers is Deuteronomy, which means "review." Basically, Moses spent a large block of time recapping the wilderness journey so that the people of Israel would learn from the past and prepare to obey in the future.

As we draw near to the end of our study, take some time to recap your own spiritual journey by drawing a timeline in the box provided on the next page. You can start from childhood or any meaningful point on your spiritual journey. Choose from the following elements as you revisit some of the blessings and difficulties in your life, drawing these simple graphics in your timeline:

ILLUSTRATION KEY FOR TIMELINE

Influential People	Exciting Times	Difficult Times	Big Decisions	Restorative Times

SPIRITUAL JOURNEY EXAMPLE

Grandma took me to her church.	My parents' divorce made me question God.	Moved away from home for college.	A friend invited me to church.	Joined a small group Bible study.	Made the decision to follow Christ.	Went on my first mission trip.	Moved for a job and got involved in outreach.

MY SPIRITUAL JOURNEY

What are some "glimpses of grace" or spiritual blessings that stand out from your timeline (even if they came through difficult seasons of life)?

Sometimes our blessings can be difficult to see. Often it is not until we have the benefit of hindsight that we recognize God's gracious hand. Some blessings are physical, such as the land flowing with milk and honey that God promised to His people. Houses, cars, clothing, and food are gifts from the Lord that many of us enjoy. Most often, however, our blessings involve character, growth, and intimacy with the Lord and people. While material blessings are temporary and bring us fleeting pleasure, spiritual blessings are eternal; and contentment is one of the spiritual blessings the Lord longs to give us—longs to give *you*. You and I can learn contentment as we thank the Lord for His gifts and obey His commands.

Talk with God

Take some time now to thank the Lord for all His blessings. Express your gratefulness for what He has done, is doing now, and will do in your future!

Today's Scripture Focus

Numbers 36

DAY 5: CONTENTMENT LEGACY

The people of Israel stood on the edge of the Promised Land with many battles still ahead. Many of us are right there with them; we can identify with believing God's promises but not yet having seen all of them fulfilled. We stand somewhere between, "Thank you, Lord" and "Help me, Jesus!" As we come to this point with our wilderness wanderers in the last chapter of Numbers, it is fitting that we find a discussion that includes women and legacy!

As you consider those who will come after you, what are some words that you hope will be associated with your legacy?

We can choose to set an example of pursuing a life of contentment that will have an effect on those in our sphere of influence for generations to come.

Though we all are still works in progress, we know that both complaining and contentment are contagious. Rather than setting an example of complaining, we can choose to set an example of pursuing a life of contentment that will have an effect on those in our sphere of influence for generations to come.

Read Numbers 36:1-13 and summarize briefly:

The people involved:

The problem:

The proposed solution:

Extra Insight

The Year of Jubilee occurred every fifty years beginning on the Day of Atonement. During this year, any land or possessions that had been sold were returned to the original owner according to Leviticus 25:8-22.

This situation reminded the people that everyone will get their inheritance. Everyone is included in the blessing. The legacy of Zelophehad will not be blotted out because he didn't have sons. In Numbers 27, we saw that these daughters (Mahlah, Tirzah, Hoglah, Milkah, and Noah) had appealed to Moses regarding their father's inheritance. Without a son, no one would inherit land, and these girls would be displaced. Moses sought the Lord, and it was agreed that the girls would inherit land once the conquest of the land was finished so that they would carry on their father's name.

Here in Numbers 36, we see that the tribal leaders brought up the problem this exception created. If they married men from different tribes, the land would pass from one clan to another . So they gave the additional guideline to the daughters of Zelophehad to marry within their own tribe. One thing I love about the leadership we find here is the solution-oriented way of handling the situation. Often leaders are tempted to not make exceptions for fear of problems arising such as this or fear of setting a precedent. But rather than lead with rigidity, Moses consulted the Lord about every decision. This is a key to contentment that we've seen throughout our study.

Doing things our own way, based on human logic or emotions, does not lead to a satisfying life. Instead, we must lean into the Lord at every turn. Whether it's a time of deliverance, preparation, uncertainty, obedience, opposition or blessing, we discover contentment by living in close intimacy with the Lord. No matter the circumstances, we must cling to God and look to Him for direction in order to make decisions that will bring lasting calm rather than quick and temporary fixes.

We've seen this principle illustrated in some of Moses' good choices and even more prevalently in the wrong choices of the wilderness wanderers, who struggled to fix their eyes on the Lord. As Warren Wiersbe points

We must cling to God and look to Him for direction in order to make decisions that will bring lasting calm rather than quick and temporary fixes.

out, "they often looked back and glorified Egypt; they looked around and compared and complained about their circumstances; and they looked within and magnified their own desires."[9]

We can't judge the Israelites too harshly, because we also have wandering eyes that get us into trouble when we look back, around, and within. We don't want to get stuck in our own wilderness wanderings of sin and lack of direction. Instead, we want to enter into the blessing of God's promises. And as we saw on Day 3, often this will mean fighting for truth, purity, and for each other in their battles!

We've learned from the first generation of Israelites, who did a lot of grumbling, that growing old doesn't always mean growing up. Age is not always a guarantee of maturity. So, we must continue our quest to learn contentment even as we are surrounded by a culture crying out for more of the things that don't satisfy. We won't do it perfectly, but we can learn from the warnings of the wilderness story in order to avoid repeating Israel's mistakes.

In the New Testament we find a succinct summary of their journey given by a disciple named Stephen as he testified before a council.

Read Acts 7:30-45 and answer the following questions:

Who did God say that He was? (v. 32)

What did Moses receive? (v. 38)

What was the response of the people of Israel? (v. 39)

What did the people carry with them in the wilderness? (v. 44)

These same life-giving words that Moses received are for us. These past six weeks we've had a long journey unwrapping culture and wading through differences in the old and new covenants. I hope we're all walking away with some principles, applications, and adjustments of attitude so what was said about the Israelites refusing to listen will not be said of us!

Let's take a few moments to review what we have learned and ask the Lord to bring to mind any additional areas of focus where we can learn contentment in our daily lives.

Read through the following summary chart, and then put a star beside the week that resonates most strongly with you during this season of your life:

Week of Study	Main Themes	Reflection Questions
1. Content in Deliverance Exodus 1–15	The people of Israel had grown accustomed to slavery. When Moses interceded for their release and life got harder, they wanted to give up. The Lord is our Deliverer, but He doesn't always rescue us in the way that seems best to us. God calls us to trust Him and cooperate in His divine plan for long-term blessings even when new challenges continually arise in life.	What would you like to be rescued from right now? Whether it's a job, situation, disease, or person, ask the Lord to give you eyes to see His timeline of deliverance. Where is the Lord calling you to cooperate with action steps along the road to freedom?
2. Content in Preparation Numbers 1–10	The Israelite nation counted its most precious resource: people! We too can take stock of what the Lord has provided in relationships. We found getting organized with a good plan can replace chaos with contentment. The Israelites followed God's light and stopped for rest. We learned that to live in the light is to live intentionally, especially in seasons of preparation. God has good plans ahead, and He calls us to get ready!	Who are the people the Lord has placed in your life to journey alongside? How can you appreciate and express your gratitude for them? Where is the Lord calling you to put things in order to help life run more smoothly in your day-to-day activity? Seasons of preparation aren't always the most exciting, but they are necessary as we get things ready for the next step of blessing ahead.

Week of Study	Main Themes	Reflection Questions
3. Content in Uncertainty Numbers 11–14	Life can be scary! The scouts saw giants and felt like grasshoppers when they checked out the Promised Land. We too can get our eyes off God and onto difficult circumstances. Their complaining was contagious, and ours can be as well; so we must vigilant to learn contentment. The people also asked for meat and got it, but it came with a plague. We must be careful in our pursuit of more that we do not obtain our desires only to find a leanness in our souls.	What challenging circumstances are you facing right now? Where is God calling you to trust Him in faith rather than give in to fear? As you consider what you lack right now—people, resources, money, health—what are you asking God to give you? Ask Him to develop your character, rather than just adjust your comfort, so that you can enjoy a rich relationship with God!
4. Content in Obedience Numbers 15–20	The Lord gave His people tangible reminders to help them learn to obey Him. Whether tassels on their clothes or an altar cover or a budding staff, He wanted them to learn to make right choices. He also made a way for their purification, knowing they wouldn't always get it right. God expects our obedience as well, but He sent His Son to cleanse us once and for all by His blood.	Where is the Lord calling you to demonstrate complete obedience? Is there a habit you need to give up or a spiritual discipline you need to pursue? What tangible reminders will help you remember to obey God's Word and live according to His plan rather than your own? Take a moment to thank the Lord for the sacrifice of His Son on your behalf so that you can be cleansed and set free from the penalty and power of sin.

Week of Study	Main Themes	Reflection Questions
5. Content in Opposition Numbers 21–26	The land flowing with milk and honey was occupied by enemies for the people to overcome. In the same way, we often have to fight to embrace God's good gifts in our lives. The wilderness wanderers battled impatience, greed, immorality, and idolatry. We often war against these same temptations. An attitude of gratitude is our greatest defense against these contentment killers.	What is standing in the way of your peace and contentment lately? Where have you seen God's blessings even in the midst of persistent opposition? What are some things you are thankful for that the Lord has been doing in your heart and mind over the course of this study?
6. Content in Blessings Numbers 27–36	Contentment doesn't mean we never express concern or appeal for change. The Lord listened to the pleas of His people and sometimes gave a green light; other times He told them to accept their consequences. As the people prepared to enter the land of blessing, they were given a review of all they had learned. God wanted them to pour out their blessings rather than just manage them. He called them to learn from the past so they could walk the path of contentment in their relationship with Him.	What blessings is the Lord preparing you to receive? How can you learn from past mistakes to set a new course for the future? What blessings have you been hoarding or managing rather than pouring out so that the world may know God? How do you see God's faithfulness as you reflect on your spiritual journey?

How do the themes of the week that you starred echo into your current circumstances?

Now write below a few brief responses to the reflection questions listed for that week (right column of the chart):

Although our study of Numbers has come to end, learning contentment will last a lifetime. I pray the Lord will continue to teach us to be satisfied with His provision no matter what our circumstances in life look like. We will need each other for support as we fix our eyes on God rather than looking back, around, or within. I'd like to leave you with five ideas for next steps to continue growing in contentment over the next weeks and months:

1. Ask God for help. We can't do it on our own. When we honestly tell God that we are struggling, He comes to our rescue and transforms us from the inside out.

2. Renew your mind regularly. Isaiah 26:3 tells us that God will keep in perfect peace those whose minds are fixed on Him. Scripture memory is a great tool to realign our thoughts with God's!

3. Worship often. You weren't intended to live for yourself—for your own comfort—or even just to survive. You were designed to live for God's glory. We will never find contentment apart from our purpose of worship.

4. Use tangible reminders. Wear a piece of jewelry, make a sign, or choose a reminder that you will see regularly. God often had His people set up monuments to remember important spiritual truths.

5. Stay connected in spiritual community. Remember that complaining is contagious, but so is contentment. Let the loudest voices in your life be those that point you toward Christ.

I'm proud of you, my friend! You persevered and made it through an often neglected book of the Bible, and I know you are richer spiritually for it. Together we've discovered more of our incredible God, who is holy, merciful, faithful, and truly more than enough. I pray that you will always look to Him to fill the ache inside you, keeping your focus on His provision and purpose in the midst of all the joys and pains of your life. His blessings await you in the promised land of contentment!

> "May the Lord *bless you*
>   *and protect you.*
> May the Lord *smile on you*
>   *and be gracious to you.*
> May the Lord *show you his favor*
>   *and give you his peace."*
> (Numbers 6:24-26)

Talk with God

Spend some time praising God and listing all the reasons you have to be content in Him today. Celebrate all that God has done in you through this study!

Digging Deeper

Have you ever wondered how the Lord was consulted by the priests? When they inquired of the Lord in that day, how did they know His answer? The priest had an ephod that contained something called the Urim and Thummim. Check out the online Digging Deeper article for Week 6, "The Special Vest" (see AbingdonWomen .com/NumbersDigging Deeper) to learn more.

Contentment Clue Word: **Share**

We learn contentment by pouring out our resources on others.

James 1:17 – All good gifts come from God

God knows we will only find contentment when we _____ _____ our blessings rather than _____ them.

Genesis 12:2-3; Deuteronomy 4:5-8; and Luke 4:25-27 – God's heart for the nations; we are blessed to be a blessing

In order to be content with our blessings, we need to make _____ to the Lord a priority.

Hebrews 9:12 – Jesus is the perfect and final sacrifice

Romans 12:1-2 – We are to offer our lives to God

Malachi 3:10 – God promises to bless our offerings

_____ what God has done.

Deuteronomy 4:9-10 – *Be careful not to forget what God has done*

We need to _____ for each other.

Proverbs 31:8-9 – *Speak up for those who cannot speak for themselves*

VIDEO VIEWER GUIDE ANSWERS

Week 1

character / circumstances
harder
leaning
restful availability
do / find

Week 2

people
flexibility
preparation
rest

Week 3

seriousness
criticism
occupied

Week 4

help
comparison
disobedience

Week 5

Attitude
patience
look / Christ
enslave / control
Godliness / Contentment
strength

Week 6

pour out / manage
offerings
Remember
fight

DIGGING DEEPER
WEEK 1 PREVIEW

THE NAMES OF GOD

See AbingdonPress.com/NumbersDiggingDeeper for the full article and other Digging Deeper articles.

In Old Testament times, the meaning of a name carried much greater weight than today. In a book about God's names, Kay Arthur writes, "In biblical times a name represented a person's character. God's name represents His character, His attributes, His nature. To know His name is to know Him."[1] Throughout the Book of Numbers, we encounter several of God's names that reveal His character.

Yahweh or Jehovah

Most often in the Book of Numbers we find God referred to as the Lord (see Numbers 1:1). In many translations, whenever the Lord appears in capital letters, it refers to the name Yahweh. The name Jehovah, which many people are familiar with, is actually based on a misunderstanding of how to pronounce the Hebrew word *Yahweh*. The Hebrew language is written with consonants on the main line of text, while the vowels are mostly represented as a series of marks above or below the consonants that help readers pronounce the words. The word *Yahweh* is written as YHWH, with vowel marks above and below. But because of a longstanding tradition that the name Yahweh was too sacred to pronounce, medieval Jewish scribes avoided using the true vowels for that name and substituted the vowels for the word *adonai*, which means "lord." Earlier Christian readers did not recognize the intention, and thought the proper pronunciation was "Yahovah," or Jehovah. Most biblical scholars believe that the word was originally pronounced Yahweh.[2]

Whether we use Yahweh or Jehovah isn't as important as understanding God's character behind His name, the Lord. *Strong's Concordance* cites the Hebrew word YHWH meaning, "the existing One." God is referred to as the Lord over 350 times in the Book of Numbers and over 6,000 times in all of Scripture.[3] This name reveals that He is self-existent; He was not created and is outside the limits of time. His character is revealed in this name as a God who is holy, set apart, unlike us. We can trust Him as the Lord who is greater and higher than we are. When trials, fears, or simply the doldrums of life are threatening to steal your contentment, you can run to Yahweh for safety.

We find many names of God that are compounded with Yahweh or Jehovah throughout the Old Testament, giving greater insight into the nature of the God we worship, such as Yahweh-Yireh (Jehovah Jireh), "The LORD will provide" (Genesis 22:14), and Yahweh-Nissi (Jehovah-Nissi), "The LORD is my banner" (Exodus 17:15).

El

Another name in the Book of Numbers that reveals God's character is El. This generic term for God that is used ten times throughout Numbers means, "God, god-like, mighty one."[4]

Elohim

The plural form of El is Elohim (or Elohiym), and this name is used twenty-three times in the Book of Numbers.[5] Elohim is the name of God used in the story of Creation. While scholars debate the reasoning for the plural, Elohim reveals God's majesty and power as ruler of the earth. It's interesting that in the creation story of Genesis 1, the verbs associated with Elohim are singular. This supports the idea that Elohim is a way of referring to the nature or character of the one God. Some other names of God that reveal His character are also compounds with the name El.

El Shaddai

El Shaddai is found in Numbers 24, verses 4 and 16. This name for God means the "all-sufficient One."[6] When the Spirit of God came upon Balaam the seer, he used the name El Shaddai in reference to the God who brought blessings on His people when others wanted God to curse them. God desires for us to see that He is all-sufficient to meet our needs.

El Elyon

El Elyon means the "Most High God," [7] emphasizing God's strength and sovereignty above all creation—including all heavenly beings. It is also found in Numbers 24:16 when God is blessing His people through Balaam. God reveals that He is mighty and powerful to help us.

Adonai

Adonai, which means "my lord," [8] functions more as a title than a divine name. It is the title of reverence that Moses uses as he intercedes for the people when God wants to destroy them in Numbers 14:17. He humbly calls on Adonai, the Lord with total authority. Then he asks God to remember His unfailing love, forgiveness, and slowness to anger. As we approach God as Adonai, we must remember He has the power to do as He desires; but like Moses, we can ask for mercy and appeal to God's love and grace.

There are many other names in the Old Testament that reveal God's character. By studying God's names, we can know Him better; and as we know Him more, we can love and trust Him more. The more we know and embrace God's character, the more content we will be in focusing on Him rather than on our ever-changing circumstances.

1. Kay Arthur, *Lord, I Want to Know You: A Devotional Study on the Names of God* (Colorado Springs, CO: Waterbrook Press, 2000), 3.

2. For more on this subject, see "Is Jehovah God's True Name," Michael L. Brown, https://askdrbrown.org/library/jehovah-gods-true-name.

3. "Yehovah," http://www.biblestudytools.com/lexicons/hebrew/kjv/yehovah.html.

4. "El," http://www.biblestudytools.com/lexicons/hebrew/kjv/el.html.

5. "Elohim," http://www.biblestudytools.com/lexicons/hebrew/kjv/elohiym.html.

6. Arthur, 37.

7. "Elyown," http://www.biblestudytools.com/encyclopedias/isbe/god-names -of.html.

8. "Adonai," http://www.biblestudytools.com/encyclopedias/isbe/adonai.html.

Notes

Week 1

1. John MacArthur, *Exodus and Numbers, The Exodus from Egypt* (Nashville, TN: Thomas Nelson Books, 2008), 14.
2. Ibid., 15.
3. Kay Arthur, *Lord, I Want to Know You* (Colorado Springs, CO: Waterbrook Press, 2000), 55.
4. Ibid., 37.
5. Frank Ely Gaebelein, *The Expositor's Bible Commentary, Volume 2* (Grand Rapids, MI: Zondervan, 1990), 287.
6. Charles F. Aling, *Egypt and Bible History: From Earliest Times to 1000 B.C.* (Grand Rapids, MI: Baker Book House, 1981),106.
7. Ibid.
8. MacArthur, 27.
9. L. R. Knost, *InHumanity: Letters from the Trenches* (Little Hearts Gentle Parenting Resources, forthcoming).

Week 2

1. Dennis T. Olson, *Numbers: Interpretation: A Bible Commentary for Teaching and Preaching* (Louisville, KY: John Knox Press, 1996), 1.
2. Ibid., 15.
3. Warren W. Wiersbe, *Be Counted: Living a Life that Counts for God* (Colorado Springs, CO: David C. Cook, 1999), 17.
4. Roy Gane, *The NIV Application Commentary: Leviticus, Numbers* (Grand Rapids, MI: Zondervan, 2004), 496.
5. Olson, 13.
6. Ibid.
7. Wiersbe, 20.
8. Elisabeth Elliot, *The Path of Loneliness: Finding Your Way through the Wilderness to God* (Grand Rapids, MI: Baker, 2001), 128.
9. Gordon J. Wenham. *Numbers (Tyndale Old Testament Commentaries)* (Downers Grove, IL: InterVarsity Press, 1981), 29.
10. Ibid., 84.
11. Gane, 504.
12. Wiersbe, 28.
13. Olson, 17.
14. Wenham, 97.
15. Gane, 532-533.
16. Ibid, 538.

17. Ibid., 540.

18. Wenham, 102.

19. Gane, 540.

20. John Trent and Gary Smalley. *The Blessing: Giving the Gift of Unconditional Love and Acceptance* (Nashville, TN: Thomas Nelson, 2011), 201.

21. Wiersbe, 20.

22. Wenham, 63.

Week 3

1.   "'anan," Brown, Driver, Briggs, and Gesenius, "The KJV Old Testament Hebrew Lexicon," http://www.biblestudytools.com/lexicons/hebrew/kjv/anan.html.

2.   Roy Gane, *The NIV Application Commentary: Leviticus, Numbers* (Grand Rapids, MI: Zondervan, 2004), 580.

3.   Richard A. Swenson, MD, *Contentment: The Secret to a Lasting Calm* (Colorado Springs, CO: NavPress, 2013), 15.

4.   "Malé," Brown, Driver, Briggs, and Gesenius, "The NAS Old Testament Hebrew Lexicon," http://www.biblestudytools.com/lexicons/hebrew/nas/male.html.

5.   Charles H. Spurgeon, *The Complete Works of C. H. Spurgeon*, Vol.5, *Sermons 225 to 285*, #244, "The Bed and Its Covering" (USA: Delmarva Publications, Inc., 2013), https://books.google.com/books?id=PmvHBgAAQBAJ&pg=PT280&lpg=PT280&dq=If+I+had+a+little+more,+I+should+be+very+satisfied.'+You+ma.

6.   Gane, 583.

7.   Warren W. Wiersbe, *Be Counted: Living a Life that Counts for God* (Colorado Springs, CO: David C. Cook, 1999), 65.

8.   Gane, 583.

9.   Swenson, 129.

10. Abraham Joshua Heschel, *God in Search of Man: A Philosophy of Judaism* (New York: Noonday, 1955), 416.

11. Gane, 593.

12. Ibid., 591.

13. Swenson, 86.

14. Packer as quoted by Swenson, 128.

15. Dennis T. Olson, *Numbers: Interpretation: A Bible Commentary for Teaching and Preaching* (Louisville, KY: John Knox Press, 1996), 78.

16. Gane, 600.

17. Wiersbe, 73.

18. Max Lucado, *When God Whispers Your Name* (Nashville, TN: Thomas Nelson, 1994), 44

19. D. L. Moody as quoted by Wiersbe, 81.

20. Ibid.

Week 4

1. J. R. R. Tolkien, *The Fellowship of the Ring* (London: Unwin Paperbacks, 1985), 324.
2. Roy Gane, *The NIV Application Commentary: Leviticus, Numbers* (Grand Rapids, MI: Zondervan, 2004), 622-623.
3. Ibid., 633
4. Frank Ely Gaebelein, *The Expositor's Bible Commentary, Volume 2* (Grand Rapids, MI: Zondervan, 1990), 835.
5. Gaebelein, 837.
6. Warren W. Wiersbe, *Be Counted: Living a Life that Counts for God* (Colorado Springs, CO: David C. Cook, 1999), 91-92.
7. Gane, 645.
8. Gaebelein, 859.

Week 5

1. http://www.desiringgod.org/messages/george-muellers-strategy-for-showing -god.
2. Warren W. Wiersbe, *Be Counted: Living a Life that Counts for God* (Colorado Springs, CO: David C. Cook, 1999), 128.
3. Gordon J. Wenham, *Numbers (Tyndale Old Testament Commentaries)* (Downers Grove, IL: Inter-Varsity Press, 1981), 191.
4. "Just a Little Bit More," Starwinar.com, https://starwinar.wordpress.com /daily-short-story/just-a-little-bit-more/.
5. Roy Gane, *The NIV Application Commentary: Leviticus, Numbers* (Grand Rapids, MI: Zondervan, 2004), 700.
6. Wiersbe, 139.
7. Phyllis Bottome, *Alfred Adler: Apostle of Freedom* (London, England: Faber & Faber, 1939), 56. http://www.goodreads.com/quotes/18069-it-is-easier-to-fight -for-one-s-principles-than-to.
8. Gane, 723.
9. Ibid., 719.
10. Dennis T. Olson, *Interpretation, A Bible Commentary for Teaching and Preaching Numbers* (Louisville, KY: Westminster John Knox Press, 1996), 156.
11. Wiersbe, 152.
12. Gane, 736.
13. Paraphrased from Olson, 157.

Week 6

1. Warren W. Wiersbe, *Be Counted: Living a Life that Counts for God* (Colorado Springs, CO: David C. Cook, 1999) 154.
2. Gordon J. Wenham, *Numbers (Tyndale Old Testament Commentaries)* (Downers Grove, IL: InterVarsity Press, 1981), 215.
3. Wiersbe, 165-166.

4. Roy Gane, *The NIV Application Commentary: Leviticus, Numbers* (Grand Rapids, MI: Zondervan, 2004), 772.
5. Wenham, 179.
6. Wenham, 249.
7. Gane, 785.
8. Dennis T. Olson, *Numbers: Interpretation: A Bible Commentary for Teaching and Preaching* (Louisville, KY: John Knox Press, 1996), 187.
9. Wiersbe, 183.

Dig Deeper into Scripture and Find Inspiration with Other Bible Studies and Books by Melissa Spoelstra

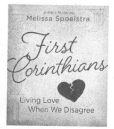

First Corinthians: Living Love When We Disagree
Participant Workbook – ISBN: 9781501801686

Learn to show love when we disagree without compromising our convictions.

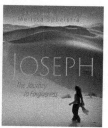

Joseph: The Journey to Forgiveness
Participant Workbook – ISBN: 9781426789106

Find freedom through forgiveness.

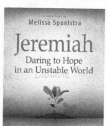

Jeremiah: Daring to Hope in an Unstable World
Participant Workbook – ISBN: 9781426788871

Learn to surrender to God's will and rest your hope in Him alone.

Total Family Makeover: 8 Practical Steps to Making Disciples at Home
Paperback Book ISBN: 9781501820656

Discover a practical approach to helping your children learn what it means to be followers of Jesus.

Total Christmas Makeover: 31 Devotions to Celebrate with Purpose
Paperback Book ISBN: 9781501848704

Connect your family more deeply with Christ during the holiday season.

DVD, leader guide, and kit also available for each six-week study.

Discover samples of her books and Bible studies at AbingdonWomen.com/MelissaSpoelstra.

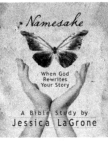

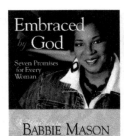
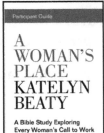